beginnings
the spiritual life

Habits of the Heart
A Participant's Companion

Andy Langford, Mark Ralls,
and Rob Weber

Abingdon Press / Nashville

Beginnings: The Spiritual Life
Habits of the Heart: A Participant's Companion

Copyright © 2006 by Abingdon Press

All rights reserved.

No part of this work may be reproduced or transmitted in any form or by any means, electronic or mechanical, including photocopying and recording, or by any information storage or retrieval system, except as may be expressly permitted by the 1976 Copyright Act or in writing from the publisher. Requests for permission should be addressed in writing to Permissions Office, 201 Eighth Avenue, South, P.O. Box 801, Nashville, Tennessee 37202-0801, faxed to 615-749-6512, or e-mailed to permissions@abingdonpress.com

New Testament Scripture taken from the HOLY BIBLE, TODAY'S NEW INTERNATIONAL VERSION®. TNIV®. Copyright 2001, 2005 by International Bible Society. Used by permission of Zondervan. All rights reserved.

Old Testament Scripture quotations in this publication, unless otherwise indicated, are from the *New Revised Standard Version of the Bible*, copyrighted© 1989, Division of Christian Education of the National Council of the Churches of Christ in the United States of America. Used by permission. All rights reserved.

This book is printed on acid-free, elemental chlorine-free paper.

ISBN 0-687-05861-9

Contents

Introduction   5

Welcome!   7

1. Where Is the Spirit in Spirituality?
   Introduction to the Spiritual Life   13

2. How Much Am I Willing to Risk?
   The Spiritual Habit of Courage   29

3. What Is Most Important to Me?
   The Spiritual Habit of Loving   45

4. Can I Find Balance in a Whirlwind World?
   The Spiritual Habit of Centering   61

5. What Do I Want to Be When I Grow Up?
   The Spiritual Habit of Simplicity   77

6. How Do I Keep My Possessions From Possessing Me?
   The Spiritual Habit of Giving   91

7. How Do I Get Ahead?
   The Spiritual Habit of Serving   109

8. Can I Go Deeper Without Going Under?
   The Spiritual Habit of Trusting   123

9. What Do I Do With My Doubts?
   The Spiritual Habit of Questioning   139

10. Can a Change in Me Change the World?
    The Spiritual Habit of Engaging   155

11. What Next?   169

Citations   175

Introduction

This book is a resource for participants and leaders in local congregations that are offering *Beginnings: The Spiritual Life*. This resource is used in conjunction with *Beginnings: Video Resources*, a set of video presentations that begin the dialogue, and *Beginnings: Participant's Guide*, a workbook for program participants.

Welcome!

"Where do we come from? Who are we? Where are we going?"
Paul Gauguin

Andy and his wife Sally were visiting the Museum of Fine Arts in Boston. A special exhibit displayed the work of Paul Gauguin. Gauguin, as Andy vaguely remembered an old lecture on art, was a nineteenth-century French artist who painted tropical scenes. As they explored the exhibit, Andy gained a new perspective about Gauguin. This artist had grown up immersed in the rigid European culture of his day. Escaping France, Gauguin fled to the South Pacific island of Tahiti for a simple life closer to nature and God. In his new setting, Gauguin created impressionistic paintings that revealed a world of bright colors, beautiful people, and an unspoiled natural order. At a deeper level, Gauguin was also on a spiritual quest. His most famous set of paintings is titled "Where do we come from? Who are we? Where are we going?" These are basic spiritual questions much like the ones we will explore together in this book. Gauguin, Andy discovered, was not just a great painter. He was a spiritual inquirer.

In our own way, we are all spiritual inquirers. Each one of us is seeking to understand the basic contours of life in communion with God and other people. Women and men, young and old, newcomers to Christianity and lifelong followers of Jesus Christ are asking,

Habits of the Heart

Where have I been? Where shall I go? Who am I called to be along the way? These questions are at the heart of every spiritual quest.

This study responds to one primary question common to all seekers, "How can I live a spiritual life?" In writing *Beginnings: The Spiritual Life,* we—Andy, Mark, and Rob—believe that Christianity provides some new directions to this basic question all spiritual inquirers ask. We assume that you already have some basic knowledge about Christianity. You possess some insights about Jesus Christ, the Bible, prayer, and other foundations of the Christian faith. All of these topics and more were the subject of *Beginnings: An Introduction to Christian Faith,* the first study in this series. Yet, being a follower of Jesus Christ involves more than just knowing the basic beliefs of Christianity.

Having begun to follow Jesus Christ, you now seek answers that involve spiritual matters. Christians believe that you discover deeper spirituality and strengthen your relationship with God through a few basic habits. These spiritual practices begin to answer your existential questions and orient your life toward Jesus Christ. You have the potential to demonstrate Christ-like patterns of life, which we call habits of the heart.

HABITS OF THE HEART

"Ask questions from your heart and you will be answered from the heart." *Omaha Proverb*

HABITS OF THE HEART introduces the personal characteristics, qualities, and virtues of men and women who follow Jesus Christ in their quest to understand and connect with their spiritual selves. As you ask foundational spiritual questions, this study will help you discover ways of living that reveal a richness of life you may never have known. You are on a journey, which, if you adopt the right habits, can lead you further and deeper in your walk with God.

Welcome!

What are these habits of the heart that will lead you further in your spiritual quest? Think of them as you might think of "heart healthy" foods on a restaurant menu. Many menus are filled with tasty but unhealthful food options. Many of us have eaten more than our fair share of French fries covered with cheese sauce to be dipped into a ranch dressing as an appetizer to a full meal! Some restaurants, however, add to their menus little red hearts — ♥♥ — beside certain foods. This heart symbol indicates foods, such as a green salad, that may be better nutritionally. Eat these foods, and your body will rejoice!

The truth, unfortunately, is that our selfish, chaotic, unbalanced, complex, and materialistic world offers us many unhealthful options for living our lives. Our modern society daily teaches us habits that lead us in the wrong direction, away from God and other people. Christians believe, however, that Jesus Christ offers his followers an alternative set of habits. Throughout HABITS OF THE HEART, we share some of the basic spiritual, heart-healthy characteristics of a Christian life—courage, love, balance, simplicity, generosity, service, engagement, trust, and even doubt—that point you toward a better road. It may be time for you to set aside the junk food of life for some spiritual health food!

> *"And here is my secret, a very simple secret. It is only with the heart that one can see rightly; what is essential is invisible to the eye."*   Antoine de Saint-Exupery

These spiritual habits are not new. Jesus Christ himself exhibited these core characteristics. Followers of Jesus Christ, both ancient and modern, have discovered that by observing these same habits, they connect with God and their neighbors. Christians have also discovered that these habits are not a human achievement, but that the Holy Spirit offers these habits as gifts. The possibility now is that you may begin to observe these spiritual habits and become more like Jesus Christ.

Habits of the Heart

"Everyone should carefully observe which way his heart draws him, and then choose that way with all his strength."
Jewish Proverb

THE SPIRITUAL JOURNEY

In the movie *The Two Towers*, based on the book by J.R.R. Tolkien, the hobbit Samwise Gamgee speaks to his companion Frodo Baggins about their journey to destroy the ring of power. Their journey was a spiritual journey for both Sam and Frodo, along with their other companions in the ring fellowship. Sam's words may echo your own concern about the meaning of life in a chaotic and sometimes evil world. Sam speaks:

> "It's like in the great stories, Mr. Frodo. The ones that really mattered. Full of darkness and danger they were. And sometimes you didn't want to know the end, because how could the end be happy? . . . But in the end, it's only a passing thing this shadow. Even darkness must pass. A new day will come. And when the sun shines, it will shine out the clearer. Those are the stories that stayed with you, that meant something. . . . Folk in these stories had lots of chances of turning back, only they didn't. They kept going because they were holding onto something."
>
> "What are we holding onto, Sam?" Frodo Baggins replies.
>
> Sam answers, "That there's some good in this world, Mr. Frodo. And it's worth fighting for."[1]

In the midst of your questions, in the midst of the darkness of our modern world, Christians believe that there is good in the world worth fighting for, worth risking your life for, and worth organizing your life around to bring forth light. The real freedom in your life is the liberty God gives you to choose to refrain from bad habits and to adopt some better habits of the heart. The Holy Spirit is at work

Welcome!

enabling you to risk following Jesus Christ and offering you love, balance, simplicity, generosity, service, trust, and other habits that allow your spirit to soar. As you look for ways to find a center in your own life, God, through the Holy Spirit, looks for ways to share with you exactly the spiritual virtues that you need to have a life that is whole. Let us together begin this journey toward spiritual wholeness.

---

1. From *The Two Towers* © MMII New Line Productions, Inc., screenplay by Walsh, Boyens, Sinclair, and Jackson.

One: Where Is the Spirit in Spirituality?

Introduction to the Spiritual Life

"Holy Spirit, giving life to all life ... you are our true life, luminous, wonderful, awakening the heart from its ancient sleep."
                                         Hildegard of Bingen

"Then Jesus was led by the Spirit into the wilderness."
                                         (Matthew 4:1)

SPIRITUAL HUNGER

Walk the aisles of most major bookstores and you may not find a section on "Christianity" or even "Religion." Instead, more frequently you will find an aisle labeled "Spirituality" with countless books on meditation, self-discovery, and a smorgasbord of religious topics. Check out the event announcements in your local paper and you may find discussion groups on the Tibetan Book of the Dead, yoga for spiritual people, and divinations. Your neighbors are listening to best-selling CDs or downloaded songs of Spanish monks chanting ancient psalms. On Bourbon Street in New Orleans, amidst the bars and music halls, fortunetellers, tarot card readers, and astrologers sit beside the street and for a modest fee offer to connect people with the spirit world.

So many people are seeking guidance from a higher source. As a society, we are convinced that an authentic life—an existence that makes sense in ultimate terms—needs a spiritual orientation. Searching for congruence, authenticity, and above all a sense of deep connection drives modern culture. This searching is really not so new. Some scientists believe that there is a "God gene," that "the need for God may be a crucial trait stamped deeper and deeper into our genome with every passing generation."[1] We are living in a time when countless people are naming their spiritual hunger. Yet, many people believe that organized religion in general, and Christianity in particular, is not spiritual enough. Christians beg to differ. True Christian spirituality can satisfy your deepest cravings.

THE BEGINNING OF JESUS' SPIRITUAL SEARCH

Jesus himself, as a young man, understood that he was on a spiritual journey. When Jesus was about thirty years old, he traveled from his home village of Nazareth down to the Jordan River. At this river, which supplied most of the fresh water to his region, Jesus' cousin John was offering life-giving transformations. John was baptizing people with water and helping seekers prepare for the coming of the messenger from God. Jesus came to John and asked to be washed in the water. As the water showered Jesus' head, "heaven was opened and the Holy Spirit descended upon him in bodily form like a dove" (Luke 3:21-22). Then God spoke aloud, "You are my Son, whom I love; with you I am well pleased" (Luke 3:22).

Dripping with water and understanding his deep connection with God, Jesus was guided by the Holy Spirit out into a stony, mountainous desert just west of the river valley. Jesus stayed in that desert for forty days, going without food, praying, struggling with evil, and receiving his mission from God. When Jesus returned from the desert, he was ready to begin his ministry. Emerging from his experience, Jesus left the wilderness behind and began a three-year journey that enabled those who followed him also to fulfill their deepest spiritual yearnings to be in intimate communion with themselves, other people, and God.

Where Is the Spirit in Spirituality?

VISION QUEST

Jesus' spiritual journey into the desert was an expression of a fundamental human desire to seek meaning and purpose of life through retreats in wild places. One experience of such a spiritual quest is found among some original peoples of North America. Native Americans from the North American plains cherish a life-directing tradition called a Vision Quest. When young people in that tradition prepare to enter adulthood, they go on a solitary retreat under the guidance of a community elder to learn their true name and discover the purpose of life. A Vision Quest may also involve an older seeker, especially in times of crisis or at a significant moment in life, who searches for wisdom and direction. The Vision Quest is characterized by several days of fasting and guided prayer. The goal is to reach union with the Great Spirit. In the quiet of this spiritual pilgrimage and retreat, the Spirit speaks the seeker's true name and gives guidance. Through this ritual of prayer, fasting, and attentiveness to God, the seeker returns from the quest with a vision of how life may be lived in a new way.[2]

"To go on a vision quest is to go into the presence of the great mystery."　　　　　　　　　　　　　　　　　　*Lakota Proverb*

A spiritual quest is a journey from one place in our interior lives to a place not yet seen. Yet, such quests also involve outward expressions of life. Responding to a profound need for direction, we seek new dimensions, directions, and seasons of life that reveal themselves in our everyday activities. We may travel north and south, east and west, and oftentimes seem to end up at the same place from which we began. When we return from the journey, we may look the same on the outside, but on the inside we are new persons who see familiar objects and persons in a whole new way. Even more so, when we return, we begin to exhibit new exterior habits and experience life in a new way. The transformation from our old self to a new self has begun.

"Listen to your life. Listen to what happens to you because it is through what happens to you that God speaks.... It's in language that's not always easy to decipher, but it's there powerfully, memorably, unforgettably." Frederick Buechner

Such a journey is a common expression of basic humanity. You may remember other stories of such journeys: the Greek hero Odysseus sailing home from the Trojan War, the knights of the Round Table seeking the Holy Grail, the English pilgrims journeying to Canterbury Cathedral, the little girl Dorothy walking down the yellow brick road to get back to Kansas, Star Wars' Luke Skywalker flying through space to save the old republic of planets, and the hobbit Frodo on his quest to destroy the ring of power. The labyrinths or mazes found in European cathedrals, and now throughout the United States, are additional symbols of such spiritual journeys and even allow one to go on the journey without traveling more than a few yards. The scholar Joseph Campbell believed that all literature may be understood through the lens of such journeys. Jesus Christ and his first band of followers were also on such a quest.

Are you on a spiritual quest? All of us are seeking to discover our true spiritual selves and develop habits in our lives that draw us closer to our God who created us and connect us more closely with the people around us. You too are a spiritual child of God being led, like Jesus, by the Spirit of God!

WHAT IS THE HOLY SPIRIT?

The name Christians provide for the Spirit of God that guided Jesus and all people in their spiritual quests is the Holy Spirit. Many people imagine the Holy Spirit as some "thing" mysterious, inaccessible, and distant. Some contemporary images describe the Spirit as an undefined, raw power that drifts through the universe, such as "The Force" in the Star Wars movies. Other people imagine the host of airy beings in the Harry Potter books or envision the

Where Is the Spirit in Spirituality?

wispy spirits that emerge when people die in movies. How do Christians define that which seems indefinable, yet is so vital in the spiritual journey?

> *"The Force surrounds us; it penetrates us; it binds the universe together."* Obi-Wan Kenobi

When the Bible speaks of the Holy Spirit, these holy words describe the personal, spiritual presence of God. This spiritual presence first appears in the ancient poetry of Genesis, the first book of the Bible. When the earth was in its infancy—"a formless void," and "darkness covered the face of the deep" (Genesis 1:1-2)—God was intimately present, loving creation into existence through the Spirit. Like a mother caressing her child's cheek, "the spirit of God swept over the face of the waters" (Genesis 1:2). The scene was equally personal when God created human beings. God gathered dust from the earth, molded the clay into human form, and then gently breathed the Spirit into the first human (Genesis 2). Like a master potter, God shaped human beings out of the earth and literally breathed them into existence. Without the Spirit of God, nothing but chaos would reign.

In Hebrew, the language of the Old Testament, the word used for God's Spirit is ruach. Ruach means spirit, breath, wind, and foundation of life, a sign of a supernatural, dynamic, creative, transforming, and unpredictable presence. [The "Spirit" of God appears ninety-four times throughout the Old Testament. For an exhaustive study of the Spirit of God see *Bible Key Words, Volume III*, by Gerhard Kittel (Harper and Brothers, 1960); pages 1–119.] This Spirit of God gave wisdom to Job, a man who sought to understand his suffering (Job 27:3). David, the great king of Israel, was filled with the Spirit (1 Samuel 16:13). The prophet Isaiah, therefore, believed that the coming Messiah of Israel would especially exhibit the Spirit (Isaiah 11:1 and 42:1).

Habits of the Heart

When we were created, God breathed into us the breath of God's own Spirit, or as Job wrote: "The spirit of God has made me, / and the breath of the Almighty gives me life" (Job 33:4). Our very creation means that we already share a fundamental spiritual connection with God. God's Spirit is not some distant mystery but an intimate presence within us from the moment of our creation. We are never isolated individuals; we are always infused with God! God has already brought the Spirit close to us, as close as our next breath.

"You need not cry very loud. God is nearer to us than we think." Brother Lawrence

Most of the time, you may glide along the surface of your life unaware of your deep spiritual self and connection with God. The noise and demands of daily distractions make it hard to imagine the possibility of such an intimate connection with God. Yet, our quest for spirituality gets beneath our surface concerns to something more essential. Our yearning to connect with the Spirit recovers an already-present awareness of our link with God.

"At the back of our brains, so to speak, there is a forgotten blaze or burst of astonishment at our own existence. The object of . . . the spiritual life is to dig for this submerged sunrise of wonder." G. K. Chesterton

JESUS CHRIST—CHILD OF THE SPIRIT

Christians believe that Jesus Christ experienced this shared intimacy with the Spirit of God in a unique way. The New Testament books of Matthew, Mark, Luke, and John, which describe Jesus' life on earth, make clear his deep connection with the Spirit. According to the story of Jesus' conception, the Holy Spirit conceived Jesus in union with a young woman called Mary of Nazareth (Matthew 1:20). When John baptized Jesus in the Jordan River, as described earlier, the Spirit descended on Jesus, like a dove" (Matthew 3:13-17).

Throughout his ministry, Jesus Christ's special connection with God through the Holy Spirit continued (Luke 11:20). Often, as in his initial desert sojourn, Jesus removed himself from the company of people to be in prayer and commune privately with the Spirit of God. When Jesus was crucified on the cross, he released his Spirit back to God and breathed his last (John 19:30). Then, God's Spirit descended upon Jesus' corpse, resurrecting Jesus Christ to new power and life (John 20). Throughout his life, Jesus understood his connection with the Spirit of God; he was fundamentally a spiritual person.

The Spirit, however, did not make Jesus into someone other than who he already was; the Spirit guided Jesus and reminded him that he could be called God's Son. As the New Testament biographer Matthew wrote: "Here is my servant Jesus whom I God have chosen, / my beloved, with whom my soul is well pleased. / I will put my Spirit upon him, / and he will proclaim justice to the Gentiles" (Matthew 12:18, citing Isaiah 42:1-2, author's translation).

THE SPIRIT AS THE GUIDE FOR JESUS' FOLLOWERS

While Jesus depended upon the Holy Spirit to assist in his ministry, even more so the followers of Jesus needed the Holy Spirit. Jesus introduced his friends to the Holy Spirit in response to a desperate plea from one of his followers. Philip, one of those first twelve followers, had grown frustrated by his inability to experience the same kind of relationship with the Spirit of God that Philip saw in Jesus. Jesus explained that even though he would ascend to God after his death and resurrection, he would not leave his friends desolate, promising "another Guide to help you and be with you forever" (John 14:16, author's translation).

In an extended conversation with his followers (John 14–16), Jesus gave the Holy Spirit a new name: *parakletos* (John 14:16).

Translations of this strange word include "comforter," "advocate," "defender of a cause," "counselor," "patron," "friend," "helper," "intercessor," and "mediator." Another good descriptive word for the "Holy Spirit" is "Guide." Because this word is closely related to spiritual quests, we will use it throughout this book.

Jesus Christ's giving of the Spirit Guide culminated in a dramatic moment between the resurrected Christ and his closest followers. On the day of his resurrection, Jesus appeared before his friends in the small room where they had been hiding from the leaders who executed Jesus. Frightened for their lives, these followers were paralyzed by fear. Jesus Christ, back from the dead, "breathed on his friends and said, 'Receive the Holy Spirit' " (John 20:22, author's translation). Re-enacting the original creation of human beings when God breathed the Spirit into the dust of the earth, Jesus' new act made possible a new life and an even deeper intimacy with God. The Holy Spirit, in this new genesis moment, was now also understood as the Spirit of Christ.

CHRISTIANS TODAY AS PEOPLE OF THE SPIRIT

Jesus Christ's gift of the Guide extended to all his followers: past, present, and future. John, who baptized Jesus at the Jordan River, had announced that he was washing people with water. John also preached that the coming Messiah from God would baptize with water and the Holy Spirit (Matthew 3:11). One of the blessings of being a follower of Jesus is that all Christians now have immediate access to the Holy Spirit. Jesus did not merely experience the Spirit; he also bestowed the Holy Spirit upon all his people.

Today, every time Christians baptize a new follower of Jesus Christ, we believe that the Holy Spirit comes upon that person in a new way. Like the dove descending on Jesus at his baptism to the blessing of the Holy Spirit as Guide on that day in Jerusalem, again and again God bestows the Holy Spirit upon the people of God.

Where Is the Spirit in Spirituality?

SAILING WITH THE HOLY SPIRIT

"God provides the wind, but we must raise the sails."

Augustine

We now invite you, as part of your spiritual quest, to participate in the same kind of intimate relationship that Jesus the Son shared with those first followers. You are not a person trying to become spiritual; you are a spiritual person trying to unleash the power of God already guiding your life! Your new communion with God through the Holy Spirit may be compared to sailing.

Several years ago, Mark and his wife, Jennifer, joined two friends for a sailing trip in Washington State's San Juan Islands. Mark recalls:

> Jennifer and I had never sailed before. We assumed there was not much to sailing. It seemed that all you needed to do was simply point the boat in the right general direction, raise your sails, and lay back and enjoy the trip while the wind worked its magic. Luckily, our friend Jim knew better. Jim, an experienced sailor, constantly went over charts and made minor adjustments to our course. In addition, Jim always planned ahead. His eyes were constantly on the horizon, preparing for the wind by studying the water ahead. Wind causes small ripples that darken the surface of the water compared to those areas where there is no wind. Jim constantly looked ahead toward the "wind line" to keep our boat on course.

Can you reconnect with your spiritual self? How can you share the intimate relationship now offered to you by Jesus Christ through the gift of the Holy Spirit? How can the Holy Spirit be your Guide? Sailing illustrates how you may be attentive to the Holy Spirit in your life. Through the following three steps of Christian spirituality, you may enable the Holy Spirit to guide you in a discovery of your spiritual self.

STEP ONE: BE OPEN TO THE SPIRIT

"We are not human beings having a spiritual experience; we are spiritual beings having a human experience."
Pierre Teilhard de Chardin

First, open yourself to the possibility of the Spirit's presence in your life. You must allow the Spirit's wind to catch your sail. An attitude of openness prepares us for an encounter with the Holy Spirit. Picture a boat, mast high in the air but with sails still tucked away. The boat will not move. If the Holy Spirit is to guide us, we must open ourselves to the possibility that God desires an intimate relationship with us.

"Ask God to make you aware of divine nudges in your life. What had God said to you through recent incidents? What was God saying to you in that unexpected phone call? in that flat tire? in that moving television program? in that bout of anxiety? in that 'coincidence'"?
Tilda Norberg

Raising our sails is where the hard work of becoming spiritual begins. Our prospects seem so ordinary and the Holy Spirit so extraordinary. The first task of spirituality requires recalling God the Creator breathing the Spirit upon us at our creation and God the Son breathing the Holy Spirit on us today. The Bible is clear that all persons who follow Jesus Christ already "live and move and have our being" in the Spirit of God (Acts 17:28). With the enthusiasm of a great Guide, the Holy Spirit longs to share our life. Julian Norwich, a twelfth-century mystic, said it well: God "wants us to know that not only does God care for great and noble things, but equally for little and small, lowly and simple things as well."[3] Step one: Simply raise the sail and watch for the guidance of the Holy Spirit.

Where Is the Spirit in Spirituality?

STEP TWO: CULTIVATE THE SPIRIT

Being open to the Holy Spirit is more than just raising our sails; it also involves searching for the wind. Use the Guide you have received. Cultivate the Spirit's presence in your life by working with the wind. Often, when we feel like the Guide no longer leads us, it may be because we have stopped seeking God's direction. We may pray for really big, life-changing decisions; but we may also leave the Holy Spirit out of the small stuff of daily life. Author John Ortberg says this strategy is not so much seeking a deeper spirituality as just hunting for "inside information."[4] If we only seek God's leading when we face a major decision—whom to marry, where to live, whether to change careers—then we are not keeping our eyes on the wind line on the water. We are only looking for bits of inside information.

God makes another model available to us. Author Kathleen Norris once described a school bus driver who appeared full of the Spirit. This bus driver made the news because she had remained calm when an unbalanced man took hostage her bus full of mentally handicapped children. When asked how she managed to talk the man out of using his gun, the bus driver said, "I pray a lot."[5] Norris point out that the bus driver did not mean that she prayed a lot at that moment, influencing God to save her and the children. What she meant was that she was in the habit of praying, listening for the Spirit's guidance continually, and seeking the Guide in all the little moments of life prior to the major crisis. Her sensitivity to the Holy Spirit had gradually changed her into the kind of person who could deal with a horrible situation.

The bus driver did not just receive the Holy Spirit in that one moment; she cultivated the Spirit's presence in her life through a variety of spiritual habits. The habits of the heart in this book are some of those spiritual practices that cultivate our spiritual selves. As we love, become more simple, gain some balance, practice generosity, learn to serve, trust in God, ask questions, and change the world, we cultivate the Spirit's presence.

Spiritual practices are the habits of the heart we pursue to foster the presence of the Guide in ourselves. Spiritual "practice" means just what it says. In the same way that a tennis player seeks to grow more proficient by working again and again on the proper strokes, so we seek to experience more of the presence of the Spirit by performing the acts over and over that reorient us to God. Spiritual practices may include reading the Bible each evening before bed or spending time in prayer each morning. Yet, spiritual practices may also be spontaneous and occasional. Turning off the television, walking a secluded beach or a scenic mountain trail, or gazing up at the night sky may help us work the wind and get in touch with our true selves. The rest of this book describes some of these basic habits that guide us closer to God.

Such spiritual practices do not need to be difficult, but they are habits that involve discipline. Woody Allen, the filmmaker and comic, observed that "eighty percent of life is just showing up."[6] Mostly, spiritual practice means coming to God time and time again, even when we do not feel like it, seeking a deeper relationship with the Holy Spirit. Author Lauren Winner once likened this spiritual attentiveness to piano etudes—brief musical studies designed to develop a particular skill: "You do not necessarily enjoy the etudes—you want to skip ahead to the sonatas and concertos—but if you don't work through the etudes, you will never arrive at the sonatas."[7] Spirituality also requires training in the basics. We must cultivate the Holy Spirit's presence in countless small habits.

STEP THREE: ALIGN YOURSELF WITH THE SPIRIT

Finally, with your sails raised and watching for the wind, allow the Spirit to catch you up and move you to a new location in your relationship with God. Align the direction of your life with the direction set by the Guide and head toward a new port.

Where Is the Spirit in Spirituality?

Another term for *alignment* is *finding your rhythm*. Rhythm is a funny thing; it can seem so inaccessible, so impossible . . . until you get it. Think back to the time you first learned to dance, hit a golf ball, play a musical instrument, drive a stick shift, ride a bike, chop an onion, type on a keyboard, whip an egg, or anything that required a regular, repeated motion. You performed the same awkward motion again and again and then everything fell into place. All of a sudden performing the task the right way became easier than doing it wrong. You got the sense that the rhythm was in you all along; you simply needed to practice enough times to bring it out.

Spirituality also requires such alignment and rhythm. As a follower of Christ, the rhythm of the Holy Spirit is already in us, a grace and power that will flow out if we allow it to. Spirituality is not so much about carving out the bad from our lives. Mostly, spirituality simply releases the good that is already there, unleashing the Spirit already within us. This unleashing of our natural spirit is what Christians mean when we speak of the Holy Spirit making us free. Spiritual freedom does not mean that we are free to do anything we want, but that we become free to live out our lives in the image of Jesus Christ. Christians feel free when our lives begin to mirror the attitudes and actions of Jesus Christ and end up in a port never before considered.

CAN THE HOLY SPIRIT GUIDE YOU?

"Who has seen the wind?
Neither you nor I:
But when the trees bow down their heads,
The wind is passing by." Christiana Rosetti

In his book *The Spiritual Life of Children,* Robert Coles wrote about Ginny, a young girl from a poor family who was bright, articulate, and imaginative, and who possessed a keenly developed spirituality. One day, Ginny was walking home and along the way encountered an elderly woman who seemed lost and confused. Ginny asked the woman if she needed help; the woman, with relief, responded, "If you could, that would be wonderful." Ginny discovered that the woman had been walking to visit her daughter but had become disoriented. The lost woman showed Ginny the written directions she had, and Ginny knew immediately where the woman had gotten lost and where she needed to go. So Ginny traveled with the woman, talked gently to her, listened to her as the woman spoke of the pain in her life, and guided the woman to her daughter's house. On the way home, Ginny wondered what it would be like to be old and wondered, if she were old and in need, whether God would send some kid like her to help. "Maybe God puts you here," Ginny thought, "and . . . gives you these hints of what's ahead, and you should pay attention to them, because that's God speaking to you."[8] Ginny was guided by the Holy Spirit.

SPIRITUALITY AS A HABIT OF THE HEART

"We claim the power of the Holy Spirit today to strengthen us for living fully, faithfully, and joyfully."
Reuben Job

In your spiritual quest, we invite you to move away from thinking that life is all up to you and you have to gut it out. Instead, discover the possibility of true intimacy with God through the Guide or Holy Spirit. Baptism alone did not give Jesus all he needed; the Holy Spirit had to guide him on a forty-day quest. And when he returned, Jesus was ready to begin his ministry, inviting others to join him on his journey.

You may also make such a decision to be open to the guidance of the Holy Spirit because the Spirit is already with you. As a Native American prayer says:

Where Is the Spirit in Spirituality?

Be with us, Great Spirit. We are your children. We have heard you in the winds, seen you in the sunrise; we have felt your kindness in the seasons.... You are near to us as the air surrounds us and fills our lungs with life. Be with us, Great Spirit. Show us the way you would have us go![9]

We invite you, like Jesus, to go on a spiritual quest and explore the habits of the heart presented in this book. As you do, we pray that you will be caught by the rhythm of the Spirit and that it will unleash the spiritual person God created you to be.

---

1. From *Time* Magazine (October 25, 2004); page 65.
2. From *Voices: Native American Hymns and Worship Resources* (Discipleship Resources, 1992); page 81.
3. From *Revelations of Divine Love,* quoted in *Amazing Grace: A Vocabulary of Faith,* by Kathleen Norris (Riverhead Books, 1998); pages 32–33.
4. From *The Life You've Always Wanted: Spiritual Disciplines for Ordinary People,* by John Ortberg (Zondervan, 1997); pages 140–41.
5. From *Amazing Grace: A Vocabulary of Faith,* by Kathleen Norris (Riverhead Books, 1998); pages 32–33.
6. From *Spiritual Fitness: Everyday Exercises for Body and Soul,* by Doris Donnelly (HarperSanFrancisco, 1993); page 163.
7. From *Madhouse Sabbath,* by Lauren Winner (Paraclete, 2003); pages x–xi.
8. From *The Spiritual Life of Children,* by Robert Coles (Houghton Mifflin, 1990); pages 332–34. Edited for inclusive language.
9. Sister Kevin Marie Flynn, quoted in *Voices: Native American Hymns and Worship Resources* (Discipleship Resources, 1992); page 65.

Two:
How Much Am I Willing to Risk?

The Spiritual Habit of Courage

"A ship in harbor is safe—but that is not what ships are for."
John A. Shedd

As Jesus walked beside the Sea of Galilee, he saw Simon [who would later be called Peter] and his brother Andrew casting a net into the lake, for they were fishermen. "Come, follow me," Jesus said, "and I will send you out to fish for people." At once they left their nets and followed him.

When he had gone a little farther, he saw James son of Zebedee and his brother John in a boat, preparing their nets. Without delay he called them, and they left their father Zebedee in the boat ...and followed him. (Mark 1:16-20)

One day as Jesus was standing by the Lake of Gennesaret [also called the Sea of Galilee], the people were crowding around him and listening to the word of God. He saw at the water's edge two boats, left there by the fishermen, who were washing their nets. He got into one of the boats, the one belonging to Simon, and asked him to put out a little from shore....

He said to Simon, "Put out into deep water, and let down the nets for a catch."

Simon answered, "Master, we've worked hard all night and haven't caught anything. But because you say so, I will let down the nets."

When they had done so, they caught such a large number of fish that their nets began to break. So they signaled their partners in the other boat to come and help them, and they came and filled both boats so full that they began to sink.

When Simon Peter saw this, he fell at Jesus' knees. . . . For he and all his companions were astonished at the catch of fish they had taken. . . .

Then Jesus said to Simon, "Don't be afraid; from now on you will fish for people." So they pulled their boats up on shore, left everything and followed him. (Luke 5:1-11)

LIFE IS A RISK

"All of life is a risk." These were the first words that Andy heard from his scuba diving instructor. In scuba diving, you put a tank of breathable, compressed air on your back and descend deep into the ocean. Andy's daughter, Ann Green, convinced him to learn this intimidating sport so they could dive together on a family vacation. So Andy went to his local dive shop and learned quite a bit about both scuba diving and risk.

Andy recalls,

> On the day of our first dive into the ocean, I had to sign a release form that stated: "I understand that scuba diving can lead to serious injury and death." The instructor told me, rather obviously I thought, that when I was in the water, there was always the danger of drowning. This wisdom did not help me overcome my fear
> Even worse, I have seen the movie *Jaws* many times. I have never been interested in having a large sea creature bite me. To relieve my fears my instructor told me, "Almost all sharks, with a few exceptions, are more afraid of us than we are of them." Having said this, he continued, "But never assume what sharks will do. They are quite unpredictable." In other words, sharks are usually safe creatures, except for the sharks that happen to be dangerous. Was this information meant to be helpful? Yet, into the water I went.

How Much Am I Willing to Risk?

All of life is a risk: a toddler taking his first steps; a youth deciding on a college; a young adult pursuing a new career; a bride and groom saying, "I do"; walking away from a destructive relationship; a widow deciding she can "make it on her own." At every stage of life, there are crossroads and intersections dividing the known from the unknown. Stepping into the unknown can be frightening. Many persons avoid risk because of this fear. You too may choose to play it safe, "to err on the side of caution." Sometimes this attitude of caution is appropriate. Not every risk is worth taking. Yet, when it comes to things that really matter—such as love, friendship, and faith—the benefits of risk outweigh the costs of caution.

> "To laugh is to risk appearing the fool. To weep is to risk appearing sentimental. To reach for another is to risk involvement. . . . To love is to risk not being loved in return. To live is to risk dying. But risks must be taken, because the greatest hazard to life is to risk nothing. The people who risk nothing . . . may avoid suffering and sorrow, but they cannot . . . change, grow, love, live. . . . Only a person who risks is free."
>
> *Anonymous*

The Guide may now lead us into the spiritual habit of courage. What does courage have to do with spirituality? Everything! Spiritual growth implies change. Change calls for risk. And, every risk worth taking requires courage. Each path on our spiritual quest begins with a step into the unknown. Only by developing the courage to take this step again and again will we move from where we are to where we long to be.

PEOPLE WHO RISKED

The first followers of Jesus were two sets of brothers, Andrew and Simon (later to be called Peter), James and John. They were all fishermen. Each day they would wake before dawn, walk the rocky paths down to the sea, unroll their fishing nets, and try their luck. Putting food on the table, paying taxes, and supporting their families all depended on this familiar routine.

One morning, Jesus interrupted their routine. When he appeared on the shore, the four fishermen recognized him at once. Jesus was the powerful teacher who had spoken with such authority. He had said, "The time has come. Open your hearts and believe" (Mark 1:15, author's paraphrase). These fishermen were not sure what Jesus had meant, but somehow his words were already coming true. A small seed of courage was beginning to take root, opening their hearts to something new.

"Take a risk and follow me," Jesus called from the shore. Immediately Andrew and Simon dropped their nets and followed. When Jesus extended the same invitation to James and John, they too made an immediate response. In the blink of an eye, the brothers stood by Jesus' side, wide-eyed and dripping wet from the Sea of Galilee. James and John left their boat—and the life that went with it—behind them, casting their fate upon Jesus' abrupt invitation.

THEN THERE WAS ZEBEDEE

Yet, James and John were not the only people in the boat that day. Scripture reports that "they left their father Zebedee in the boat . . . and followed [Jesus]." As James and John ran to meet Jesus, we are allowed a final backward glance at the one who was left behind. Four sprang to their feet. One hesitated. Four dropped their nets. One was not quite ready to let go. Zebedee had an opportunity to change his life. What held him back? Why did he refuse to take the risk? Perhaps Zebedee was simply afraid.

COCOONING

"Any real change implies the break up of the world as one has always known it . . . the end of safety. And at such a moment,

How Much Am I Willing to Risk?

unable to see and not daring to imagine what the future will now bring forth, one clings to what one knew, or thought one knew; to what one possessed or dreamed one possessed."

James Baldwin

Fear comes in all shapes and sizes. A child who cannot sleep may be afraid of the dark. A professor whose palms sweat on the way to the podium may fear public speaking. A fiancé who breaks off an engagement may be afraid of commitment. A soldier who paces back and forth before battle may fear injury or death. In its purest form, however, fear reveals simply an internal alarm system. Fear, warning you of impending threats, has proven to be a very useful feeling. Fear protects you from unexpected dangers and foolish risks.

Yet, sometimes fear gets in the way. Fear may keep us from taking risks we should take. When this hesitation happens repeatedly, fear becomes an unhealthy habit that paralyzes our spiritual growth. We call this habitual fear "cocooning." A caterpillar in its shell remains safe and secure, but cocoons are meant to be temporary. Eventually the cocoon of self-protection becomes suffocating. Cocoons are made to be broken by the spread of a butterfly's wings. So also the Holy Spirit needs to break our cocoon for us to grow in our spiritual quest. If we always remain where we feel comfortable and safe, we may have spun a cocoon that prevents us from spreading our spiritual wings.

FEAR OF CHANGE

Two closely related fears lead to the unhealthy habit of cocooning: fear of change and fear of failure. Fear of change springs from feelings of insecurity. Everyone needs a certain amount of security to have peace of mind. Our sense of security is rooted in familiarity. Security comes from our daily routines that are comfortably predictable; from old friendships and family ties with established bonds of trust; from investments that are guaranteed by the government; and from the confidence that the future will unfold in an expected way. All of these firm foundations offer great blessings. The abrupt decisions of Andrew and Simon, James and John are so remarkable because of their willingness to leave behind such security. Jesus called them out of the familiarity of their secure patterns of life, and they responded immediately. They left their homes, their businesses, and their families to follow him.

Yet, these foundations also make Zebedee's hesitation easier to understand. Zebedee had spent much of his life building up his little fishing business. He probably hoped to pass the family business down to his sons James and John. This way of life was all he had ever known. Life was secure.

Mark reflects,

> I can relate to Zebedee. I too have been known to sit in the boat a while and mull things over. It took me two and a half years of college to declare a major and four years of dating to pop the question. One of my longest periods of indecision came in graduate school. I pursued a doctorate after seminary, planning to become either a professor or a pastor after graduation. I do not want to admit how long this stage of my life lasted, but let's just say it was beginning to look like my graduation party would have to double as a retirement party! One of my college friends told me that I took those televised public service announcements to "stay in school" a little too literally.
>
> There seemed no end to the ways I could put off finishing my dissertation. First, I switched degree programs, adding another year of coursework. Then, I decided to spend an extra year studying in Germany. Whatever I did, I never felt sufficiently prepared to leave school and begin my vocation. I realize now that I was compensating for feelings of insecurity. I was afraid to take the next step. Though I was tired of living off measly stipends and student loans, my life was comfortably familiar. I knew how to be a student. I was not so sure I could say the same about anything else.

Perhaps Zebedee felt too insecure to follow Jesus. If this is true, we understand his hesitation. But his reluctance to get out of the boat was still a shame. Insecurity leads to spiritual paralysis. When we feel insecure, we cling to the familiar behaviors, possessions, and beliefs that make us feel comfortable. Security is a wonderful, even necessary, part of life, but when it prevents us from becoming the person we were meant to be, we are trapped in a cocoon of our own making.

FEAR OF FAILURE

Beyond the fear of change, another paralyzing fear is the fear of failure. This fear springs from feelings of inadequacy. Inadequacy may arise from past disappointments and the sense that we are not in control of our own destiny. We believe that other people or forces or situations write the script of life; and unless we are very cautious, we may be scripted to fail. When fear of failure takes hold, we enter the unknown more tentatively. We find ourselves paralyzed and unable to proceed with even the most positive changes in our lives.

In Arthur Miller's play, *Death of a Salesman,* Willie Loman is a man with a deep fear of failure. The play ends tragically at Willie's funeral after he has committed suicide. Willie's son Biff stands by Willie's grave reflecting on his father's life. Biff remembers that his father loved working with his hands and longed to be a craftsman. But, Willie Loman never pursued his dream. Instead, Willie lived the life of a traveling salesman—an occupation that did not suit him at all—because he was afraid of failure. "He had the wrong dreams," Biff laments. "The man didn't know who he was."[1]

Perhaps what kept Zebedee in the boat was his fear of failure. He knew only fishing and was afraid to try anything else. Such fear too is understandable. Everyone has made compromises in the name of fear: not trying out for the team, not asking out a person on a date, not applying for another job, not changing addresses, not listening to the voice of God. Yet, playing it safe has its own dangers. If we avoid risk at all cost, we never discover who we really are. We will not grow spiritually or reach our full potential. Like an old car left in the yard, we will begin to rust—in this case, from the inside out.

> *"I realize that if I wait until I am no longer afraid to act, write, speak, be, I'll be sending messages on a ouija board, cryptic complaints from the other side."* — Audre Lorde

The classic term for cocooning in Christian spirituality is *attachment*. The word *attachment* comes from old European roots meaning "staked" or "nailed to." Attachment tethers our heart to fears that hold us back from what we were meant to become. What makes us feel secure and safe may also leave us trapped, suffocating in our own cocoon. Attachment may even lead us to become like Zebedee. We, too, may choose to stay in the boat—attached to all that is secure and safe—even when the Son of God appears on the shore.

THE SPIRITUAL HABIT OF COURAGE

> *"It is the belief in a power larger than myself and other than myself which allows me to venture into the unknown and even the unknowable."* — Maya Angelou

How does the Guide free us from our spiritual cocoon? Jesus' answer is straightforward. He invites us to follow him into the unknown. Jesus once said, "I am the gate for the sheep . . . whoever enters through me will be saved. They will come in . . . and find pasture" (John 10:7, 9). The Holy Spirit, in many ways and on many occasions, enables us to encounter Jesus. Especially at crossroads in our lives, Jesus Christ invites us to leave behind false securities and safety zones so that we may enter a realm of new possibility. All that Jesus requires is walking through the open gate. Yet, we must risk taking that first step into the unknown: a risk that calls for courage.

How Much Am I Willing to Risk?

Courage is often confused with the bravado of "fearless" adventurers: jumping off high cliffs or running through walls of fire. Yet, courage is not about being fearless. The word *courage* derives from the French word *coeur* for "heart." This connection between heart and courage seems appropriate. Courage is not the absence of fear but the presence of love. If we love, we take risks for our beloved. We face great difficulties without losing heart. A courageous person hears the cautions of fear, yet responds with her heart. She chooses to act in spite of fear. Courage is seen in the everyday heroism of persons who love greatly— spouses, friends, children, and parents. At these moments of challenge, the Guide helps us discover the deepest commitments of our heart. These unique moments of decision give us the courage to step into the unknown. Author Mark Collins tells of such everyday courage in the life of a friend named Henry:

> Twice each week, Henry... takes two buses ... to see his wife at the Kane Nursing Home in the South Hills of Pittsburgh. His wife has Alzheimer's. Despite fifty-two years of marriage, she doesn't know Henry from Adam. He's just another nice face in the room. . . . But this nice face washes her twice a week, making sure to run a towel between her toes so she won't chafe. He turns her ... to dab some A&D ointment on a stubborn bedsore. He combs her hair and always complements her long white locks—the same locks that first attracted him fifty-two years ago. . . .
>
> He talks to her about their life together. . . . To her, these stories of youth and marriage and children are dreamy and senseless. Sometimes she cries for no reason, and he holds her. . . . On those days . . . the bus trip home is long and sad. But he'll be back on Thursday, smiling as if nothing happened. . . .
>
> Twice a week, Henry risks his life. He risks everything that's ever meant anything to him: the corporate memory of their five decades together; his children's inheritance, whittled away by private nurses and co-payments; his sense of himself as Annie's husband, when really he's become Annie's

parent.... He's living on the edge... [with] no helmet,... no safety net....
Next Thursday, Henry will come once again aboard the 16C Bellevue, the first leg on the adventure of a lifetime."[2]

> *"Courage doesn't always roar. Sometimes courage is the little voice at the end of the day that says, 'I'll try again tomorrow.'"*
>
> Mary Anne Radmacher

Courage, like fear, comes in all shapes and sizes. Yet, unlike fear, courage dares to step into the unknown. How can we begin to develop the spiritual habit of courage in our own lives? The image of the cocoon again helps. If we have ever witnessed the rebirth of a butterfly, we have seen the cocoon slowly begin to break apart. A small portion of the butterfly emerges. Finally, the butterfly spreads its wings, leaving its cocoon behind. Taking a risk with God has a similar movement. First, a tiny crack appears in our self-protective cocoon. Then, we step out into the unknown of God's possibility. Finally, we spread our wings and begin to become the person God is calling us to be.

BREAKING THE COCOON

> *"And the day came when the risk to remain tight in the bud was more painful than the risk it took to blossom."*
>
> Anais Nin

Our spiritual cocoon begins to break apart the moment the Spirit enables us to confront whatever is holding us back. This confrontation calls for reflection on how we respond to risk and fear. Part of this process is acknowledging the message of Andy's scuba diving instructor, "All of life is a risk." If safety and security are our ultimate goals, this message contains terrible news. But, if we are ready to embark on a spiritual adventure—to pursue our quest with the Holy Spirit—the invitation offers great news. If all of life is a risk, we might as well risk our lives on what is most important to us. The choice is not between safety and risk. The choice is between those risks that are worth taking and those that are not.

Patty Hansen, co-author of the popular book *Chicken Soup for the Soul*, wrote this little fable about risk and fear.

> Two seeds lay side by side in the fertile spring soil. The first seed said, "I want to grow! I want to send my roots deep into the soil beneath me, and thrust my sprouts through the earth's crust above me. . . . I want to unfurl my tender buds like banners to announce the arrival of spring. . . . I want to feel the warmth of the sun on my face and the blessing of the morning dew on my petals!" And so she grew.
>
> The second seed said, "I am afraid. If I send my roots into the ground below, I don't know what I will encounter in the dark. If I push my way through the hard soil above me I may damage my delicate sprouts. . . . And if I were to open my blossoms, a small child may pull me from the ground. No, it is much better for me to wait until it is safe." And so she waited. A yard hen scratching around in the early spring ground for soil found the waiting seed and promptly ate it.[3]

It seems counterintuitive, but avoiding the unknown is just as risky as embracing it. We have the power to choose those risks that are worth taking. Once we make this choice, courage rises up inside us from the deep places of our heart.

RECONSIDERING OUR FEARS

When the cocoon begins to break, the second part of this process requires reconsidering our fears. We may feel so well acquainted with our fears that we are convinced we know all about them. Yet, we may be too close to our fears to see them clearly. Fears often become distorted. They seem larger and more powerful than they really are. Occasionally, we need to take a step back from our fears and reconsider them for what these fears really are.

Habits of the Heart

Jane Stern suffered from a lifetime of paralyzing phobias about illness and death. One day, she came up with a surprising solution. She volunteered as an emergency medical technician. In an interview with *U.S. News and World Report,* Jane explained, "I thought, 'I have to do the scariest thing I can think of. If I can do it, then I will be OK.' And the scariest thing for me—as a raging hypochondriac [a person who is irrationally fearful of illness]— ... was to sit in the back of closed ambulance with a dying person.... There hasn't been a day when my pager goes off that I don't get a rush of panic and think 'I can't do this.' Then I do it and I'm OK." Jane concluded, "Fear is a hologram. It seems so real until you test it, and then it falls apart and there's nothing there. It's getting the nerve to test it that's hard."[4]

Our spiritual cocoon begins to break apart when we realize that the Guide gives us the power to choose our risks, and we come to understand that the fears that hold us back are empty holograms, destined to fall apart the moment we dare test them.

STEPPING OUT

Finally, having stepped out of our cocoon and faced our fears, we must step into the unknown. The first step is always the most difficult. Perhaps this is why the ancient Chinese philosopher, Lao Tzu, reminded his students that "a journey of a thousand miles must begin with a single step."[5] If we fail to take this first step, our adventure never begins.

Some of the most magnificent cathedrals in Europe were built progressively, over decades or even centuries, without benefit of blueprints or architects. What a risk for a small village to lay that first stone in the middle of an empty field! Yet, if that first stone had not been placed, the grand cathedral would never have been realized.

The same is true for our relationship with God. Every great spiritual adventure begins with a single step. As a young adult, Kumar

How Much Am I Willing to Risk?

left his family in India and moved to Seattle, Washington. Faced with loneliness and career setbacks, Kumar longed for his life to change. He was ready to step into the unknown. One day, while sitting in his cubicle at work, he whispered a prayer of desperation and courage: "I am willing to take on anything you lead me to, even if it's difficult or dangerous. But I am willing to take the risk if you will show yourself to me." As he drove home from the office, Kumar met a woman in a gas station. She invited him to an evening worship service at her Presbyterian congregation.

During the service, Kumar found himself feeling much the way the very first followers of Jesus probably felt the day they encountered Jesus at the Sea of Galilee. Kumar's heart began opening to the possibility of something new. He said, "That night when I went home, I felt something changing all through my body. Since I'm a software guy, I thought, 'Some new program is running inside me.' ... When I came out of my room, my roommate said to me, 'Kumar, you look different.' I said, 'Well, I think I'm going to become a Christian.'"

Life flows through us when we risk stepping out, charting a new course and sailing off into the unknown for a spiritual adventure with God. Yet, God does not draw up a detailed blueprint, spelling out how the adventure will unfold. Instead, God promises that the Holy Spirit will accompany us on our journey that begins with a single step.

SPREADING YOUR WINGS

"The glory of God is the human being fully alive."
Saint Irenaeus

Spread your wings! Something unexpected happens when we step into the unknown. We discover a deeply familiar place once hidden beneath our fears. When Jesus Christ invites us to follow him, he also invites us to discover our true self—the person God created us to be. Jesus once said, "I have come that they may have life, and have it to the full" (John 10:10). As we risk accepting this invitation again and again, we discover something in ourselves that we never knew was there. The great irony of the spiritual life is that we are most fully ourselves only when we are open to change and risk. This openness is what it means to spread our wings.

In his South African presidential commencement address, Nelson Mandela, the leader of the anti-apartheid movement in South Africa, spoke of the courage to become your true self:

> Our deepest fear is not that we are inadequate. Our deepest fear is that we are powerful beyond measure. It is our light, not our darkness, that most frightens us. We ask ourselves, who am I to be brilliant, gorgeous, talented and fabulous? Actually, who are you NOT to be? You are a child of God. Your playing small does not serve the world.... We were born to make manifest the Glory of God that is within us. ... And as we let our own light shine, we unconsciously give other people permission to do the same. As we are liberated from our own fear, our presence automatically liberates others.[7]

RISK TO FOLLOW

We do not know what happened to Zebedee, but we do know that Jesus Christ calls us countless times throughout our lives. Perhaps one day, Zebedee overcame his fears and climbed out of the boat. Throughout this book, we invite you to follow the example of the very first followers of Jesus. Learning to love, serve, give, simplify, trust, question, and develop all the spiritual habits of the heart will be a risky enterprise. But, we believe the benefit of these risks will greatly outweigh their costs.

Andy recalls what happened when he finally worked up the courage to go scuba diving with his daughter and dove into the ocean:

How Much Am I Willing to Risk?

I saw some marvelous sights in that undersea world! Floating in the crystal blue water, watching coral of every color of the rainbow, and swimming among vast schools of fabulous fish was spectacular. I saw a sea turtle, a moray eel, huge lobsters, fish as large as myself, thousands of conch shells, and even manatees. I overcame my fears by taking a risk. I now know that I have just begun to explore a new world beneath the waves.

---

1. From *Second Innocence: Rediscovering Joy and Wonder: A Guide to Renewal in Work, Relationships, and Daily Life,* by John Izzo (Berrett-Koehler, 2004); page 25.
2. From *On the Road to Emmaus: Stories of Faith, Doubt and Change,* by Mark Collins (Liguori Publications, 1994); pages 105–07.
3. From *Chicken Soup for the Soul,* by Jack Canfield and Patty Hansen (Health Communications, 1993); page 220.
4. From *You Have the Power: Choosing Courage in a Culture of Fear,* by Frances Moore Lappe and Jeffrey Perkins (Jeremy P. Tarcher/Penguin, 2004); pages 79–80.
5. From *www.worldofquotes.com.*
6. From *Finding Faith: Life Changing Encounters with Christ,* by Sharon Gallagher (Page Mill Press, 2001); pages 150–52.
7. From *In a Dark Wood: Journeys of Faith and Doubt,* edited by Linda Jones and Sophie Stanes (Fortress Press, 2004); page 141.

Three: What Is Most Important to Me?

The Spiritual Habit of Loving

"All you need is love."   *The Beatles*

On one occasion an expert in the law stood up to test Jesus. "Teacher," he asked, "what must I do to inherit eternal life?"

"What is written in the Law?" [Jesus] replied. "How do you read it?"

[The expert in the law] answered, "Love the Lord your God with all your heart and with all your soul and with all your strength and with all your mind"; and "Love your neighbor as yourself."

"You have answered correctly," Jesus replied. "Do this and you will live."   (Luke 10:25-28)

What spiritual habit of the heart underlies all the other habits? What is the goal for which you are most willing to risk your life? The answer to both questions is the same: love. From music to movies, television to novels, the Beatles were right. Love is all we really need. When the Spirit guides us to love selflessly and calls us forward in our spiritual quest, we will fill an empty place in the heart.

WHAT IS LOVE?

What is love? You would think the answer would be easy. Yet, love has so many meanings; its multiple translations often cause confusion. People use the word love to describe a wide range of sentiments for an equally wide range of beloved objects. A beautiful beach, a new car, and of course chocolate may inspire love. Bumper stickers proclaim "I ♥ New York" and "Virginia is for lovers." Andy loves Duke University basketball. Mark loves tennis. Rob loves eating in the French Quarter of New Orleans. This one word expresses the bond that unites parents to their children, the loyalty a patriot feels toward her country, and the favorite items an enthusiastic shopper brings home from the mall. What is love? When the same word is applied to both a devoted spouse and a pint of Ben and Jerry's ice cream, defining *love* becomes difficult.

> *"The Eskimos had fifty-two names for snow because it was important to them: there ought to be as many for love."*
>
> Margaret Atwood

Perhaps we can come to a more satisfactory definition if we consider those life-changing experiences that inspire us to take a great risk. Wrapping a newborn baby in our arms. Holding the hand of a dying parent. Saying "I do" at the altar. These moments call us forward into the unknown. These moments inspire us to become the person we long to be. Only in the rich soil of love can we change and grow in our spiritual quest. Andy recalls:

> I have always been in an environment where love was pervasive. My mother and father gave birth to me and nurtured me. My extended family of grandparents, great-grandparents, aunts, uncles, cousins, three brothers, and later a wife and daughters broadened the circle of love around me. My family counseled, guided, and encouraged me. On a wider scale of love, Christians throughout my life fostered, challenged, honored, and humbled me. Of course there were days when I wasn't certain about this love; and there were times when I failed adequately to respond to its presence. Nevertheless, all these loving people inspired me through their words and actions to strive to become the person that God created me to be. Love created and is creating me.

What Is Most Important to Me?

"Love as powerful as your mother's for you leaves its own mark. Not a scar, no visible sign . . . to have been loved so deeply, even though the person who loved us is gone, will give some protection forever."
                    Headmaster Dumbledore to Harry Potter

GOD AS LOVE

Love is at the center of Christian spirituality because Christians share the simple yet profound conviction that "God is love" (1 John 4:8). God creates every human being and every living creature out of love. In the first chapter of Genesis, after God's first act of Creation, Scripture proclaims, "God saw that the light was good." "It was good" is repeated five times to emphasize the effusive, exuberant love of God spilling forth in the act of creation (Genesis 1:4, 10, 12, 18, 21, 25). A nineteenth-century writer, G.K. Chesterton, compared the enthusiasm of the Creator to that of a child who never grows tired of playing the same enthralling game over and over. "It is possible," Chesterton writes, "that God says 'Do it again!' to the sun every morning and every evening, 'Do it again!' to the moon. It may not be automatic necessity that makes all daisies alike. It may be that God makes every daisy separately but has never got tired of making them."[1] God creates because God is love, and creation is the fruit of that love.

God as love becomes especially evident in the creation of human beings. God expresses a unique love for humanity, declaring humans to be not just good but "very good" (Genesis 1:31). We were created like God so that we can be in an intimate relationship with God; our very existence can be traced back to God's persistent yearning for personal companionship. God delights in our creation as a parent delights upon seeing her newborn child. Julian of Norwich, a twelfth-century Christian, said that human beings are literally "clothed" in God's love: "Our Lord... is our clothing, for God is that love which wraps and enfolds us, embraces and guides us, surrounds us.... "[2]

"The unfathomable mystery of God is that God is a Lover who wants to be loved. The one who created us is waiting for our response to the love that gave us our being. God not only says: 'You are my Beloved.' God also asks: 'Do you love me?' and offers us countless chances to say yes."   Henri Nouwen

WHY IS LOVE SO DIFFICULT?

We might reasonably ask that if we are made from love and created for the express purpose of loving, why is finding love so difficult? Why do we search for that which we already possess? Why do we sometimes feel isolated and alone? Isolation is a frustration, an ache, and a dis-ease at the center of our lives. Isolation occurs when we are not able to love as fully as we desire, when we are not able to accept love as completely as we need.

Human beings experience isolation in two very different ways. One experience of isolation is an unhealthy self-centeredness. The Bible calls this condition sin, but modern psychology uses the term *narcissism*. This word comes from the Greek myth of Narcissus. Narcissus was a beautiful young man, the son of a god and a nymph. One day, Narcissus offended a goddess, and her punishment was to cause Narcissus to fall in love with himself. Watching a still pool of water, Narcissus saw his own beautiful reflection and could never pull himself away from his own image. Narcissism is a habit of focusing only on oneself, which prevents us from casting our full attention to God and to other people. We become self-absorbed, so distracted by our own concerns that we lose sight of everyone else. Over time, this habit spoils the intimacy we were created to share with God and others. Narcissism leaves us feeling isolated and alone.

"All the lonely people, where do they all come from?"
    The Beatles

What Is Most Important to Me?

The flipside of narcissism is loneliness. Loneliness may have been the disease that caused the lawyer described at the beginning of this chapter to come to Jesus and ask his question. Because we all live in a world where self-centeredness pervades, the love you receive from other people often feels inadequate, sometimes even corrupt. That love generally comes with strings attached. As a result, we may feel that no one fully accepts us for who we really are. If narcissism is the failure to love others fully, loneliness is the disappointment of never completely receiving the love we need. Think of how we sometimes feel hurt and bruised in even the best of human relationships. Hurt as a symptom of loneliness signals our search for a more perfect love, where our true worth is recognized and we are accepted just as we are. Over time, loneliness may cause us to shrink from love. We dread another disappointment. We fear being hurt. We retreat into ourselves. Loneliness, like narcissism, leaves us feeling isolated and alone.

In Graham Swift's novel *The Light of Day,* George Webb is a heartbroken man in his early fifties. Past relationships hurt George, and he has done more than his share of hurting. One day, George senses what he has been missing all along. He longs for a completely different kind of love than he has experienced thus far. At that moment of insight, George recalls learning as a boy that "none of us is so bad, so worthless that God will let us slip through the net of [God's] love." George wonders if such a love is even possible and then reflects, "Whether God is up there or not and whether [God] has got a net I don't know, but I think it is how it ought to be.... There ought to be one other person who won't let us slip through their net. No matter what we do. No matter what we have done"[3]

You may be like George or the lawyer who approached Jesus. You may be longing for a more perfect love. This seeking is nothing to be ashamed of; God planted this yearning in our heart. Searching for love is part of our nature. We were created in the image of the God who above all else longs to love and to be loved. No wonder we yearn to experience the kind of selfless, ceaseless affection that only God can provide. No wonder we also long to share an uncorrupted love with others.

> *"You would not seek God or love God unless you had first been sought and loved.... For the love is the reason for the search, and the search is the fruit of the love, and its certain proof."*
> Bernard of Clairvaux

EXPERIENCING GOD'S LOVE

The first step beyond isolation occurs when the Holy Spirit helps us recognize God's love for us. Recognizing real love is not easy. Most of us have become used to receiving love only in its corrupted forms. God's love, however, is radically different from the love typically experienced. The Bible expresses the love God has for humanity with two beautiful words: the Hebrew word *hesed* in the Old Testament and the Greek word *agape* in the New Testament. These two words may open our heart to a new experience of love.

Hesed refers to the resilience, the persistence, and the unshakeable enthusiasm of God's affection. Hesed is often translated as "steadfast love." The Old Testament prophet, Isaiah, reflects upon "all the Lord has done for us . . ." according to the abundance of God's steadfast love (Isaiah 63:7). Author Melanie Svoboda helps us understand the kind of love Isaiah knew:

> God's apparent lack of restraint when it comes to creating things is but a symptom of a deeper "problem": God lacks restraint when it comes to loving, too. In fact, God is most unrestrained when it comes to loving. We see this... throughout the Old Testament. The Chosen People turn away from God again and again. What does God do? Does God throw up . . . divine hands in disgust and cry, "Enough already!"... No, God continues to love them, taking them back again and again and again. There is no end to God's love.[4]

What Is Most Important to Me?

Agape, the New Testament word, emphasizes the self-giving, sacrificial character of divine love. You may remember the "Love Feast" from *Beginnings: An Introduction to Christian Faith,* the first study in this series. The original name of the meal was an "Agape Feast." Agape love is all about risk. Agape risks giving of oneself without any thought of reward or personal benefit, loving persons who may not love in return. Agape goes beyond mere physical attraction, friendship, or even the deep caring of families. All the other forms of love have some measure of self-interest. Agape comes with no strings attached. Jesus described agape in his story of a father who patiently awaited the return of his rebellious, prodigal son. When the young man finally came home, the father ran out to meet him, threw his arms around his son, and restored to him the full measure of his inheritance (Luke 15:11-24). God loves you without testing your worth or counting the cost, and nothing you do can spoil the affection God feels for you.

Recall a time in your life when you experienced glimpses of hesed or agape: the countless sacrifices of a devoted parent; the steadfast patience of a teacher who never gave up on you; the persistence of a friend who walked by your side through addiction; the support of a colleague during a tough time at work; the visit of an old friend at the death of a parent; the care of a friend when a relationship ended; the exuberant kisses of a two-year-old. Remember the power and warmth of the love you received and then consider this: God's love infinitely exceeds all these expressions of love put together.

JESUS AS LOVE

These manifestations of true love point beyond the limits of our world and help us imagine the perfect love of God. Christians believe that the uniquely true sign of God's love is revealed in Jesus Christ. Christians believe Jesus Christ is God's love in the flesh. The Gospel of John begins with the beautiful proclamation that in Jesus

Christ, the word that God spoke at Creation "became flesh and made his dwelling among us" (John 1:14). Jesus Christ is hesed and agape, shaped by the Holy Spirit, in the flesh. Through Jesus Christ, God enters into the fabric of human life and reveals the true depth of divine love.

Even narcissistic emperors understand the power of Jesus' love. As Napoleon Bonaparte once wrote, "Between [Jesus Christ] and every other person in the world there is no possible term of comparison. Alexander, Caesar, Charlemagne, and I founded empires. But on what did we rest the creations of our genius? Upon force. Jesus Christ founded his empire upon love, and at this hour millions of people would die for him."[5]

The presence of Jesus Christ reminds us that even when we feel most isolated from God, we are not separated from God's love. The early Christian preacher, Paul, expresses this beautifully: "For I am convinced that neither death nor life, neither angels nor demons, neither the present nor the future, nor any powers, neither height nor depth, nor anything else in all creation, will be able to separate us from the love [agape] of God that is in Christ Jesus our Lord" (Romans 8:38-39). God's love for us is so high, so deep, and so wide that nothing we do, nor anything that any other power in the universe can do, can sever our relationship with God. The love God offers is reminiscent of a pop song from the 1960s: "Ain't no mountain high enough, ain't no valley low enough, ain't no river wide enough, to keep me away from you."[6]

SHARING GOD'S LOVE

A lawyer once approached Jesus and asked, "What must I do to experience life as it was meant to be?" Led by the Spirit, this isolated man risked stepping forward into the unknown. Yet, if he were going to risk changing his life, he had to be certain of the goal. So this lawyer asked Jesus an intensely personal question, "What should be

What Is Most Important to Me?

most important to me?" As was typical with Jesus, he responded with a personal question of his own: "What does your personal study, your own reading, your unique understanding of God indicate the answer to be?" Instead of providing a quick answer, Jesus suggested that the lawyer look deep into his own experience for the answer. As is often the case in spiritual quests, the answers we seek, we already know.

For the young lawyer, the answer was obvious. (Or did the Guide inspire him?) "Love," the lawyer said. Jesus then assured the young man, "The answer to your question, therefore, is simple. Through love you will discover the life you are looking for. Embrace love. Love God. Love others, too, even as you love yourself. Love well and you will discover life as it was meant to be" (author's paraphrase).

> *"True religion is loving God with all our heart, and our neighbor as ourselves; and in that love abstaining from all evil and doing all possible good to all."*   *John Wesley*

LOVING GOD

> *"I have long known that if I want to be happy on earth I must fall madly in love with God."*   *Carlo Carretto*

The inquiring lawyer was on the right track. He had to begin by loving God. To love God risks following the Spirit and shifting the focus of our lives away from ourselves. Turning from ourselves to another is the first step toward abundant life. The lawyer's answer echoed the ancient text from the Old Testament Book of Deuteronomy 6:4-9:

> Hear, O Israel: The LORD is our God, the Lord alone.
> You shall love the LORD your God with all your heart,
>   and with all your soul, and with all your might.

Keep these words that I am commanding you today in your heart.
Recite them to your children
   and talk about them when you are at home and when you are away....
Bind them as a sign on your hand,
   fix them as an emblem on your forehead,
and write them on the doorposts of your house and on your gates.

These words of instruction are called the Shema. The Shema is the core of Jewish faith. For thousands of years, these biblical verses have served as a reminder to the Jewish people that God reigns over every aspect of their lives—heart, soul, mind, and strength. Every bit of who we are becomes a sacred offering, dedicated to the love of God. The Shema sets this one goal as the all-consuming purpose of life.

> *"Lord, because you have made me, I owe you the whole of myself, because you have promised so much, I owe you all my being."*   Saint Anselm of Canterbury

Jews use several methods to preserve a central place in their lives for loving God and are good examples of how people may passionately demonstrate their love of God. Daily when awaking and retiring, observant Jews recite aloud this promise to love God. They place the words of the Shema in a small box on the doorpost of their homes. Before entering, they will touch the box and silently remember their pledge to love God. A copy of the Shema is also placed in a small black box with leather cords, then wrapped around a person's forehead or arm during prayer. For thousands of years, Jewish persons have performed such actions as holy habits to remind them that the promise to love God with their whole selves is the most important thing in life.

What Is Most Important to Me?

"A man is only as good as what he loves."   Saul Bellow

Andy once knew a man who risked falling in love with God. The night was cold and damp. A small, mountain congregation was having a revival, but a sudden snowstorm had kept many people away. The congregation bravely sang a few hymns, quietly heard the Bible read and proclaimed, and fervently offered prayer. Junior had come that night with his wife Maxine; he did not believe in God or belong to any community of faith. But on this night, Junior was present; he was a part of that gathering, and God's love reached out to him. Although crippled by disease, Junior arose and came forward on his crutches. Junior declared that he felt God reaching out and loving him. In response, Junior dedicated his whole life to loving God. Three weeks later, Andy baptized Junior in the waters of the Linville River. For the rest of his life, Junior developed habits that expressed his love for God. He rarely missed worship. He started a Bible study group. He spent time each morning in prayer. Junior also set aside destructive habits that distracted him from loving God. He gave up alcohol and abusive behaviors. The love of God overwhelmed Junior that night; and through his holy habits, his life and the life of his mountain community were changed.

LOVING OTHERS

"The best way to know God is to love many things."
                                                    Vincent Van Gogh

Just as important as the first commandment is the second: Love your neighbor as yourself. These two commandments fit together and make a whole response to God's hesed and agape for us. The second law quoted by the lawyer was from the Old Testament Book of Leviticus: "You shall love your neighbor as yourself" (Leviticus 19:18). The lawyer linked these two commandments together. In order to love God, you must also love other people. Jesus was very pleased with this answer. Jesus responded, "You have answered correctly. Do this and you will live."

Jesus lived this way. He expressed his love for God by loving everyone he met. Jesus became friends with the foreign woman at the well (John 4:3-29). Jesus forgave a woman who had committed adultery (John 8:2-11). Jesus touched and healed a woman who had a lifelong ailment (Mark 5:24b-29). Jesus became friends with the unlovable Zacchaeus (Luke 19:1-10). Jesus washed his disciples' feet (John 13). In all these instances, Jesus revealed how God wants human beings to love. Christians seek to model their lives after the way Jesus loved. The goal of Jesus' followers is to share with other people the perfect love of Christ—a love that is not corrupted by the selfishness of narcissism or driven by the unfulfilled needs of loneliness.

"As our heavenly Father has in Christ freely come to our aid, we also ought freely to help our neighbor, . . . and each one should become as it were a Christ to the other that we may be Christs to one another." Martin Luther

How can you begin to reveal hesed and agape to the people around you? To love as Christ loves, we must first learn to pay attention to the people around us. As we mature in love, we are no longer distracted by excessive self-concern or isolation. Instead of looking at ourselves, we are able to give others our full attention. Mark recalls sitting with a family in a nursing home while their elderly mother passed away:

The two daughters were completely focused on the frail little woman who lay motionless in bed. They were cherishing every final moment. The daughters looked deeply into their mother's eyes, smiling at her, stroking her hand. Anticipating every need, they applied a cool washcloth to her brow and chips of ice across her parched lips. For what seemed like hours, no one spoke. The daughters sat by their mother's

What Is Most Important to Me?

bed with patience and attentiveness. I was moved by the love I witnessed. Yet, I was also uncomfortably aware of how often I am distracted, how rarely I give persons my full, undivided attention.

Truly loving another person requires us to recognize that person's infinite worth. Often, you may be tempted to see only a person's relative worth based on accomplishments or possessions, talent or charm; love is then doled out to the most deserving. Alternatively, to love as Christ loves is to see the absolute value of others, recognizing that they were created out of God's own infinite love.

Mark was once sitting alone in a coffee shop in Canada. A group of young adults entered dressed in sweatshirts and jeans. Each young adult accompanied an older, mentally handicapped woman. The younger persons were obviously the caretakers of the challenged, older women. The caregivers had dressed their charges in the finest clothes. The older women wore beautiful dresses with matching straw hats and carefully applied makeup. You could see the pride the challenged friends felt in their glowing eyes. Their younger caretakers ushered them to their seats and brought them croissants and coffee. These young adults attended to their friends with obvious respect and warmth. For Mark, the memory of that day unveils a sense of what it means to truly love.

> *"God looks at the world through the eyes of love. If we ... as human beings made in the image of God also want to see reality ... as it truly is, then we, too, must learn to look at what we see with love."* — Roberta Bondi

WHO IS MY NEIGHBOR?

In Jesus' conversation with the lawyer, the dialogue went deeper. After Jesus agreed that the way to discover the meaning of life is to love God and love our neighbor, the lawyer quizzed Jesus further,

Habits of the Heart

"And who is my neighbor?" (Luke 10:29) The follow-up question was quite legitimate. Is your neighbor the person who lives next door, a colleague at work, or a citizen of your own nation? Jesus answered the lawyer's question with a story:

> A man was going down from Jerusalem to Jericho [a winding, isolated road], when he fell into the hands of robbers. They stripped him of his clothes, beat him and went away, leaving him half dead. A priest happened to be going down the same road, and when he saw the man, he passed by on the other side. So too, a Levite [another holy person], when he came to the place and saw him, passed by on the other side. But a Samaritan [a citizen of Samaria, a nation in conflict with the Jewish people], as he traveled, came where the man was; and when [the Samaritan] saw the injured man, he took pity on him. [The Samaritan] went to him and bandaged his wounds, pouring on oil and wine. Then [the Samaritan] put the man on his own donkey, brought him to an inn and took care of him. The next day [the Samaritan] took out two [silver coins] and gave them to the innkeeper. "Look after him," [the Samaritan] said, "and when I return, I will reimburse you for any extra expense you may have."
>
> (Luke 10:30-35)

Jesus then asked the lawyer, "Which of these three travelers [the two holy people or the foreign adversary] do you think was a neighbor to the man who fell into the hands of the robbers?" The legal expert knew that Samaritans and Jews were bitter enemies. They were not to speak, touch, or relate to one another. A Samaritan helping a Jew would have been as offensive to the lawyer as it would be for an al Qaeda terrorist to help a wounded United States soldier. Yet, the lawyer replied that the neighbor was the one who had mercy on the injured man. Then Jesus said to his inquirer, "Go and do likewise" (Luke 10:36-37).

What Is Most Important to Me?

"Love consists in sharing what one has and what one is with those one loves. Love ought to show itself in deeds more than in words."
                                       Ignatius of Loyola

Who are your neighbors? How do you demonstrate this love of other people? Your neighbor is everyone who needs your assistance. Every time Christians gather around a newborn baby to pray, tell a Bible story to a child, or prepare a funeral meal for a grieving family, they love one another. Serving a meal to the hungry, sheltering the homeless, repairing a neglected home, writing a letter to legislators to support foreign aid, marching through the streets for justice, or joining a mission team are ways of showing Christian love. When Christians reach beyond the divisions of race, gender, age, nationality, wealth, education, religion, sexual orientation, or any other distinction they become good neighbors.

"Love thy neighbor, even when he plays the trombone."
                                          Jewish Proverb

THE WAY OF LOVE

In the late nineteenth century, a young girl named Therese lived in France. When she was still a child, guided by the Holy Spirit, she set an unusual goal for her life. Therese decided that she would become a saint. She also concluded that becoming a saint was really quite simple, not easy, but simple. Therese called her path to sainthood "the Little Way." Therese vowed that every part of her life and every ounce of her energy would be devoted to love. She declared that love was her vocation. Therese dedicated herself to responding to everything in her life—every menial chore, every chance encounter, and every petty insult—with love. Every event, however mundane, became an opportunity to share God's love.

Therese was only twenty-four years old when she died of tuberculosis. She had spent her last years living in a convent in Liseux,

France. As she was dying, one of her religious sisters read to her about the eternal happiness waiting for her in heaven. "It is not that which attracts me," Therese replied, "It is love! To love and be loved!" Therese's message, her secret to a life of meaning and purpose, has become an inspiration to people all over the world. Thousands have adopted her "little way" of love as part of their own spiritual quest. Today, Christians all over the world remember her not as a young girl from Normandy but as Saint Therese of Liseux.[7]

Are you like the inquiring lawyer? Are you searching for something worth risking your life for? How will you discover what that "something" is? Begin by letting the Spirit help you accept God's love for you. Trust in God's hesed and agape. Embraced by that love, then risk sharing hesed and agape. Jesus' simple answer to the young lawyer is an answer for us all: Develop the spiritual habit of love. "Do this and you will live" (Luke 10:28).

---

1. From *Orthodoxy*, by G. K. Chesterton (Ignatius Press, 1995); page 66.

2. From *Showings*, by Julian of Norwich, translated by Edmund Colledge and James Walsh (Paulist, 1978); page 130.

3. From *The Light of Day*, by Graham Swift (Alfred A. Knopf, 2003); page 77.

4. From *Abundant Treasures* (Twenty-Third Publications, 2000) in *A Guide to Prayer for All Who Seek God*, by Rueben Job and Norman Shawchuck (Upper Room Books, 2003); page 25.

5. Quoted in *Evidence That Demands a Verdict*, by Josh McDowell (Here's Life Publishers, 1986); page 127.

6. Lyrics by Marvin Gaye.

7. From *Letters*, by Therese of Liseux, translated by A. Camber (Liseux, 1949).

Four:
Can I Find Balance in a Whirlwind World?

The Spiritual Habit of Centering

"What I am looking for is some sort of balance in my life—a balance 'so delicate, so risky, so creative' that it is like a bird in flight, a dancer in motion. . . . By daring to lose my balance I keep it."
Esther de Waal

As Jesus and his disciples were on their way, he came to a village where a woman named Martha opened her home to him. She had a sister called Mary, who sat at the Lord's feet listening to what he said. But Martha was distracted by all the preparations that had to be made. She came to [Jesus] and asked, "Lord, don't you care that my sister has left me to do the work by myself? Tell her to help me!"

"Martha, Martha," the Lord answered, "you are worried and upset about many things, but few things are needed—or indeed only one. Mary has chosen what is better, and it will not be taken away from her." (Luke 10:38-42)

TIME TRIALS

"Now here, you see, it takes all the running you can do, to keep in the same place. If you want to get somewhere else, you must run at least twice as fast as that!"
The Red Queen in Alice in Wonderland

Habits of the Heart

In one of the most popular episodes of the *I Love Lucy* show, Lucy and Ethyl take jobs in a candy factory. Their assignment is to wrap each individual piece of chocolate as it comes by on a conveyor belt. At first, everything goes smoothly. The candies pass at a reasonable pace. Lucy and Ethyl pick up each candy and carefully wrap it in foil. Then the machine starts going faster. The candies zip past them, one right after another. In a panic, Lucy and Ethyl resort to stuffing chocolate into their mouths, under their hats, and down their blouses. When their supervisor enters the room, she does not notice Lucy's and Ethyl's bulging cheeks or strange lumps in their clothes. All the supervisor sees is an empty conveyer belt—the sign of a job well done. "Fine! You're doing splendidly," the supervisor says. Then she calls back to the machine operators, "Okay, boys! Speed it up!"

You probably know how Lucy and Ethyl feel. We run as fast as we can, trying our best to keep up with impossible demands. Just when we think we cannot take anymore, it is as if someone yells, "Speed it up!" and life spins totally out of control.

The length of the average American workday has grown longer over the past decade. So too has the amount of time workers commute to and from their jobs, as well as the likelihood that unfinished work will be brought home to complete. In her book *The Overworked American,* Juliet Schor notes that the United States has recently surpassed Japan as the longest-working nation in the world.[1] Home life is just as harried. There is always another meal to cook, another load of laundry to sort, and another afternoon in the minivan juggling soccer practices with dance recitals. The media bombard us with images and information from television, the Internet, radio, newspapers, and wireless communicators. Understandably, we may sometimes feel our only recourse is to respond as Lucy and Ethyl did. We resolve to do everything just a little bit faster.

"We are a nation that shouts at a microwave oven to hurry up."
—*Joan Ryan*

Can I Find Balance in a Whirlwind World?

If we log onto Amazon.com in search of advice, we will see hundreds of books suggesting the same "solution" Lucy and Ethyl tried. We will see titles such as *How to Double Your Productivity* or *How to Get More Done in Less Time*. These books try to help us adapt to the hectic pace of contemporary life. Yet, what if this strategy is not the solution but part of the problem?

A DISEASE OF THE HEART

"If I had my life to live over, I would start barefoot earlier in the spring and stay that way later in the fall. I would go to more dances. I would ride more merry-go-rounds. I would pick more daisies."
Nadine Stair

God did not intend for human beings to live at the teeth-rattling speed of a bullet train. Chronic busyness is bad. High blood pressure, ulcers, weakened immune systems, and chronic fatigue are just some of the consequences of the hectic pace of contemporary life. Medical studies even suggest that constant deadlines disturb the pace of the human heart, leading directly to heart disease and strokes. The Chinese pictograph for the word *busy* is appropriately composed of the characters for *heart* and *killing*. If we adopt the relentless pace of contemporary American life, we place ourselves physically at risk.

Even worse, life at hyperspeed is also spiritually dangerous. When our lives spin out of balance, something inside of us slips out of gear. We not only risk heart disease but also a spiritual disease of the heart: a fundamental distraction from the presence of God and a frenzied existence at odds with the natural rhythm God intends for us. Our days become a blur, and the people we love and long to connect with become blurs too. When the frenzy hits, no longer does the gentle wind of the Holy Spirit lead us forward in our spiritual quest, but the chaotic bluster of a whirlwind causes us to run in circles as fast as we possibly can.

CENTERING AS A HABIT OF THE HEART

Is there is an alternative path? We do not have to spend our lives "battening down the hatches," merely responding to the whirlwind. With some practice, the Guide may assist us to develop the spiritual habit of centering. Centering allows us to focus on God even when life is a blur. Becoming focused helps us to remember the essentials even in the midst of our busyness. Centering may also help us simply to slow down. Developing the habit of centering includes three steps. First, we locate a deep, peaceful place in our soul: our center point. Second, we begin to unwind our internal clock. Finally, we discover the joy of resting and being renewed in the presence of God.

FINDING YOUR CENTER POINT

"What is at the center of your life? Carefully examine where you spend your attention, your time. Look at your appointment book, your daily schedule. . . . This is what receives your care and attention—and by definition your love."   Wayne Muller

Perhaps you remember going to a carnival as a child. Three minutes on a whirling galaxy ride would leave you so dizzy you could barely walk. Yet, a carnival worker could stand on the same ride for hours, showing no ill effects at all. Why? Strapped to the outer edge of the ride, you absorbed the full impact of its speed. The operator stood in the middle, at its center point, the one place where she was immune to its ferocious speed. Is there a center point in your life? Do you have a place where you can experience the peace of God and somehow remain immune to the dizzying effects of a whirlwind world?

This center point may also be called the heart. The ancient Hebrews of the Old Testament used the word *heart* to suggest a person's essential nature—the center of emotions, intellect, and will.

Can I Find Balance in a Whirlwind World?

Today, the word *heart* carries similar connotations. Consider the sentence, "I feel it in my heart." When we speak of our heart, we are referring to depth, power, and intimacy all at the same time. We emphasize the force of the feeling deep within us, pulsating and powerful. *Heart* also conveys intimacy, suggesting that the feeling we hold is precious to us. Our heart is our essence—the deepest, most vibrant, and intimate part of who we are, where we are warmed with joy, broken in grief, and swept away by love. The place where we long to experience God in the most deeply personal way is our center.

An early Christian preacher of the New Testament encouraged Christians to be renewed at their center point so that "Christ may dwell in your hearts" (Ephesians 3:16-17). If we are going to allow the gentle winds of the Holy Spirit to soothe the jarring effects of the whirlwind, we must locate a place of stillness and peace at the core of ourselves. Centering is about more than just altering our lifestyles; it reflects a change that happens from deep within.

> *"In every stage of my search, I've discovered . . . that Jesus Christ stands at the center of my seeking. If you were to ask me point-blank, 'What does it mean to you to live spiritually?' I would have to reply, 'Living with Jesus at the center.'"*
>
> — Henri Nouwen

A GENTLER LIFESTYLE

As a national director of Young Life, a Christian ministry for high school students, Fil Anderson loved his job but was ambivalent about his frenzied schedule. Working eighty hours a week, he felt "harried and hassled" even as he "loved being in demand." After a while, the feelings of professional success began to be outweighed by a sense of spiritual failure. He recalls, "My life was filled with doing things for God rather than pursuing intimacy with God. . . . I had confidence in my ability to do the work of God, but I was clueless when it came to letting God work in me."²

The whirlwind had been a constant force in Fil's life. As a young man, Fil had once become so overworked that he broke down physically, emotionally, and spiritually. Suffering from "utter exhaustion and depression," Fil was admitted to a mental hospital. While he recovered, a psychiatrist concluded that Fil's problem not only stemmed from his hectic lifestyle. His crisis was also rooted deep within:

> The doctor went on to talk about his missionary father, a man who spent his adult life loving God and others as he loved himself. He described the rhythm of his father's life as "graceful" and his way of treating others, and himself, as "gentle." He urged me to live the rest of my life believing God's love for me was not contingent on my performance. His final words to me were wise and true: "God will never love you any more or less because of anything you manage, or fail, to achieve."³

Years later, after several relapses into a workaholic lifestyle, Fil finally realized the wisdom of the doctor's advice. He heard the Spirit calling him not to give up his passion for his work but to work in a different way, to emulate the graceful lifestyle of the psychiatrist's missionary father. "Through my frustration and disappointment, Jesus was telling me that he wanted me to live in the world but live differently. The change Jesus was calling forth," Fil finally decided, was "a change of my heart."⁴

Many people have the strange idea that they can be truly accepted by other people only if they prove themselves to be competent, responsible, and productive. Stranger still, they believe they can begin to accept themselves only when they get their act together and become totally efficient and highly effective persons. There may be something deep inside us driving us to the outer edge of the whirlwind, so that we will finally be able to prove our worth. Fil found an alternate path, an even deeper place where he was not defined by performance or productivity. From this center point, a more gracious rhythm, a gentler lifestyle, could emerge.

"In a society that judges self-worth on productivity, it's no wonder we fall prey to the misconception that the more we do, the more we're worth."   Ellen Sue Stern

God loves us not because of what we do but because of who we are. We do not have to change or produce or perform to receive God's love; agape is already ours. When the Holy Spirit allows us to recognize God's acceptance, we no longer have to prove we are acceptable. We are free to leave the whirlwind behind. This is a change of heart, a discovery of our center point.

UNWINDING THE CLOCK

Having becoming centered, a change of heart may now lead us to think of time in a new way. The New Testament makes a distinction between two kinds of time—*chronos* time and *kairos* time. For instance, the Book of Acts reports, "Paul decided to sail past Ephesus to avoid spending time [*chronos*] in the province of Asia..." (Acts 20:16). *Chronos* is human time—measured by its duration, by the ticking of the clock or the passing of the years.

Kairos, on the other hand, is God's time. A modern understanding of kairos is closer to what we call "quality time." Kairos has to do not with the number of seconds, minutes, or even years but with the depth and power of the moment at hand. At the very beginning of Jesus' ministry, the Holy Spirit enabled him to proclaim, "The time [*kairos*] has come" (Mark 1:15). In other words, the time was somehow ripe and full. We experience kairos—God's time—when we lose ourselves in the moment, and time seems to stand still. Imagine young lovers gazing into each other's eyes, an artist absorbed in her craft, or a saint deep in prayer.

Our culture is obsessed with chronos time. Many of us are compulsive clock-watchers: We have clocks beside our beds, in our cars, and on roadside displays. When we make a purchase with our credit card, the receipt tells us the exact time of our purchase; when we arrive at work we may be clocked in; and we are often judged by our punctuality. In *Gulliver's Travels*, the tiny Lilliputians noticed Gulliver consulting his watch so often they concluded that his timepiece must be his god. One wonders what those small creatures might say about us. Mark recalls,

> While vacationing at the beach, I witnessed a young father talking on his cell phone and anxiously checking his watch while he helped his two-year-old son build a sand castle. This father was caught up in chronos time. So concerned about the passing of precious minutes, this man missed out on the depth of the experience. His obsession with time kept him from being fully present in the kairos.

"We breathe the air of a generation which, as the old phrase goes, 'takes time seriously.' People nowadays take time far more seriously than eternity."   Thomas Kelly

Part of the spiritual habit of centering is giving more attention to kairos or the quality of our time. The poet, Carl Sandburg, once said, "Time is the coin of your life [and]... it is the only coin you have."[5] The Christian faith affirms that time is a gift of God. God has given us our hours and days and our work and leisure. Time is neither a commodity to be managed nor a possession to be hoarded but a gift to be treasured, savoring each moment like a fine meal. No one will ever live in kairos completely. Yet, as we begin to strive for more kairos moments in our lives, we obsess less about the minutes constantly slipping away. Instead, we focus on those God-given moments when we can be fully present to ourselves, to those people we love, and most of all to God.

Can I Find Balance in a Whirlwind World?

RESTING IN GOD'S PRESENCE

"It is not enough if you are busy. The question is, What are you busy about?"   Henry David Thoreau.

The biblical story of Mary and Martha illustrates how to rest in God's presence. Mary and Martha were close friends of Jesus and two of his most devoted followers. One night the sisters prepared a special dinner for Jesus. Martha must have been especially concerned that everything be perfect for their guests. You can almost feel Martha's anxiety rising as she put the finishing touches on dinner: slicing the lamb, arranging the fruit, and ladling hot soup into bowls. Martha's pace was frantic, resembling an episode of *The Iron Chef*, a Food Network show in which chefs compete to prepare a gourmet meal in an hour.

It was then Martha noticed her sister Mary apparently doing nothing. Mary was sitting beside Jesus completely engrossed in what he had to say. An exasperated Martha finally blurted out to Jesus, "Do you not care that Mary has let me do all this work by myself? Tell my good-for-nothing sister to help me!"

Jesus responded to Martha, "Relax, what Mary is doing is worthwhile too." He did not tell Martha to stop preparing the meal or send out for pizza or Chinese takeout. Neither did he undercut Martha's gracious act of service. Yet, Jesus gently reminded Martha that her hectic pace had distracted her from the central purpose of their evening together. Martha was so anxious to feed Jesus that she overlooked the fact that Jesus had come into her home to feed her with his teaching.

Mary and Martha are often seen as opposite figures: contemplative versus active. Some Christians see Mary—quiet, open, and attentive to the Spirit—as a model for spirituality. Other people identify with Martha who is strong, self-assured, and pragmatic. The truth is that followers of God need both parts—the dreamer

Mary and the doer Martha, balancing out each other in our lives. Mary and Martha are not strangers and opposites but truly sisters!

> *"Believe me, Martha and Mary must be together to accommodate the Lord."* — Saint Teresa of Avila

PRACTICING THE PRESENCE OF GOD

The spiritual habit of centering is a change of the heart. This change may involve cutting back on some of our activities. More than that, however, it involves carrying out our tasks in a new way. Martha's mistake was not that she was busy but that she allowed her busyness to distract her from the presence of Jesus. Our goal may be to regain some balance between rest and activity. We need both to find moments to catch our breath physically and spiritually and to learn to rest in God's presence, even when we are in the midst of some challenging activity. This centering takes us to the eye of the hurricane, where there can be peace and calm even amid the chaos.

A French monk of the seventeenth century, Brother Lawrence, had a unique ability to be centered in each one of his activities. His example and simple writings on the subject have inspired Christians for generations. Brother Lawrence's great insight was that he could experience God's peaceful presence no matter what he was doing.

At his monastery, for example, Brother Lawrence was assigned to kitchen duty. For years, he prepared meals and washed dishes for his many Carmelite brothers. He did the work of Martha. While other monks prayed, composed hymns, or hand-copied the Bible, Lawrence labored in the kitchen. This difficult work, however, did not sever his kairos with God. Lawrence believed that scouring every pot and scrubbing every dish was an extension of his worship of God. Every morning he would pray, "Lord of all pots and pans and things . . . make me a saint by getting meals and washing up the

Can I Find Balance in a Whirlwind World?

plates!" Lawrence would tell his fellow Christians, "The time of business does not with me differ from the time of prayer; and in the noise and clatter of my kitchen, while several persons are at the same time calling for different things, I possess God in as great tranquility as if I were upon my knees."[6] In a centered life, work becomes an extension of prayer. Even in the midst of the whirlwind, the Guide helps us find the peaceful, calming presence of God.

> *"It is not only prayer that gives God glory but work. Smiting an anvil, sawing a beam, whitewashing a wall, driving horses, sweeping, scouring, everything gives God some glory if being in God's grace you do it as your duty. To go to communion worthily gives God great glory, but a man with dungfork in his hand, and woman with a sloppail, give God glory too. God is so great that all things give God glory if you mean they should."*   Gerard Manly Hopkins

SABBATH MOMENTS

The Holy Spirit can help us learn to rest in God's presence. But where do we begin? When life slips out of balance, how can we find our way back to center? The most traditional way for followers of God to find a kairos moment is by observing the sabbath. The word *sabbath* comes from a verb in Hebrew meaning to pause or to cease. Since ancient times, Jews have set aside the seventh day of each week (Saturday) for worship, rest, and renewal. The sabbath commemorates the seventh day of Creation, when God rested after creating the world (Genesis 2:2-3). Jews believe that in keeping the sabbath, they are imitating God's gracious rhythm and honoring God by returning a portion of their time to the Creator who gave life itself (Exodus 20:8-11). Christians also set a day apart. They observe a day of worship and rest on the first day of the week (Sunday) to commemorate the day that Jesus Christ was raised from the dead.

What would happen in your life if you rested, *really* rested, one day a week? You could worship, pray, cook a healthy meal, take a walk, visit with family, phone your parents, and get a good night's rest. The reality, however, is that most of us find it difficult to set apart an entire day for worship, rest, and renewal. If that is true for you, start small. Attend a worship service this Sunday. Take an afternoon of sabbath rest. Set aside a half hour just to be in God's presence. In such moments, you could pray, meditate, and read Scripture. You might even reflect on the ways the Holy Spirit has worked in your life over the past week or on where you are in your spiritual quest. Other sabbath moments—kairos moments—might include spending an hour or two in some physical activity: walking in the park, hiking, playing golf, working in your yard, or going to the gym.

Try to see your actions as an extension of your prayers, as an opportunity to experience the presence of God. Each individual action may seem inconsequential; yet something important is taking place. You will be regaining your balance, quietly shifting your focus back to center, and rediscovering the joy of feeling God's presence.

Another effective way to practice centering is to create some "sabbath moments" throughout your busy days. We can see this pattern in the life of Jesus Christ. Although Jesus was very busy—healing desperately sick people, instructing his followers, and counseling individuals—he remained intimately connected with God. The Bible describes how Jesus, often in the middle of hectic activity, went to secluded places to pray (Matthew 14:23; Mark 6:46; Luke 6:12; 9:28). Jesus' attentiveness to kairos allowed him to connect deeply with each person he encountered. He was able to be fully present in each moment because each day was shaped by small sabbath moments created by the Guide. We can imitate the gracious rhythm of Jesus' life by beginning the day with God, discovering hidden moments, locating our sacred places.

Can I Find Balance in a Whirlwind World?

SACRED PLACES, HIDDEN MOMENTS, SACRED SPACES

"We wait in the quiet for some centering moment that will redefine, reshape, and refocus our lives."   Howard Thurman

The Holy Spirit yearns to open up sacred spaces in our whirlwind world. In addition to sabbath moments, begin each day with God. As soon as you wake, spend just a moment resting in God's presence. Power comes by beginning the day with God, remembering that each new day is a gift from God to be cherished and savored. Mark has an eighty-four-year-old friend who begins each day recalling the gift of the coming hours and then "thanking God for another free twenty-four!" Simply by starting each day with gratitude, we are better able to withstand the pressures of the whirlwind.

"I met God in the morning
When my day was at its best
And God's presence came like sunrise,
Like a glory in my breast.
All day long the Presence lingered,
All day long God stayed with me,
And we sailed in perfect calmness
O'er a very troubled sea.
Other ships were blown and battered,
Other ships were sore distressed
But the winds that seemed to drive them
Brought to us a peace and rest."
                              Ralph Spaulding Cushman

Another pattern to help you center: Discover hidden moments. We can turn potentially frustrating moments—waiting in a checkout line, idling in traffic, or waiting for a late client—into opportunities to rest in God's presence. Any unexpected delay could be God's way of saying, "Remember me?" Many potentially sacred moments remain hidden by the big distractions in our lives. You probably know the familiar saying, "No one ever said from his deathbed, 'I wish I had spent more time at the office.' " To that observation we could easily add surfing the Internet, computer gaming, and watching television. (A 1998 study conducted by the A. C. Nielson Company revealed that the average American watches a total of more than fifty-two days of television per year.) Simply by cutting out frivolous time-wasters and making the most of unexpected delays, we can experience sabbath moments throughout the day.

Locate sacred spaces. Many persons have a special prayer room in their house, a place set aside for reflection and meditation. We can set this space apart simply by lighting a candle and allowing the scent and light of the flame to refocus our attention on the Holy Spirit. Remember that the symbols of the Holy Spirit throughout the Bible include flames of fire and smoke rising toward heaven. The range of other visual cues is endless. Author Veronique Vienne suggests leaving a single rose in a vase well past its prime. When the flower's head begins to droop, she is instantly reminded of the posture of prayer. This subtle cue helps turn her busy kitchen into a chamber of prayer.[7] Beyond our homes, countless sacred spaces become holy ground. Some persons place benches in their gardens to invite reflection. Still others feel God's presence in the car, suggesting that a minivan can become a monastery. One of Mark's friends never turns on the radio during her morning commute, enjoying a reflective silence with God.

Cultivating a deeper relationship with God is the most important goal of our spiritual quest. By starting each day with God as well as discovering hidden moments and sacred spaces, we reserve our most cherished time for that kairos opportunity.

A story speaks about hidden moments and sacred spaces of life. An older man had the habit of slipping into a certain chapel at the same time every day. There he would sit and apparently do nothing. A priest observed this silent visitor with growing curiosity. One day, unable to contain his wondering any longer, the priest asked the elderly man, "What do you do in there?" With a twinkle in his eye, the man simply replied, "I look at God. God looks at me. And we smile."[8]

FROM BEING DRIVEN TO BEING CENTERED

Step out of the whirlwind roaring around you. You may be so driven by the force of chronos that you spend your life running in circles. Instead, experience the gentle winds of the Holy Spirit. By discovering kairos anew, we may develop a new habit of centering. As we get in touch with the core of our selves, where we are accepted and loved by God, we can learn to be fully present in each moment of our lives and to rest in God's presence even when the winds of life are raging. As the story of Mary and Martha reveals, centering is a most difficult habit to learn. Yet, as we learn to center, a more gracious rhythm, a gentler way of life, begins to emerge.

---

1. From *The Overworked American: The Unexpected Decline in Leisure,* by Juliet B. Schor (Basic Books, 1992).
2. From *Running on Empty: Contemplative Spirituality for Overachievers,* by Fil Anderson (WaterBrook Press, 2004); pages 3, 5–6.
3. From *Running on Empty: Contemplative Spirituality for Overachievers,* by Fil Anderson; page 10.
4. From *Running on Empty: Contemplative Spirituality for Overachievers,* by Fil Anderson; page 14.
5. From *The Creative Call: An Artist's Response to the Way of the Spirit,* by Janice Elsheimer (Shaw Books/Water Brook Press, 2001); page 125.
6. From *The Practice of the Presence of God,* by Brother Lawrence (Fleming H. Revell, 1958); page 6.
7. From *The Art of the Moment: Simple Ways to Get the Most from Life,* by Veronique Vienne (Clarkson/Potter, 2002); page 87.
8. From *Running on Empty: Contemplative Spirituality for Overachievers,* by Fil Anderson; page 135.

Five: What Do I Want to Be When I Grow Up?

The Spiritual Habit of Simplicity

"In order to seek one's own direction, one must simplify the mechanics of ordinary, everyday life."   *Plato*

Then people brought little children to Jesus for him to place his hands on them and pray for them. But the disciples rebuked them. Jesus said, "Let the little children come to me, and do not hinder them, for the kingdom of heaven belongs to such as these."

(Matthew 19:13-14)

" 'Tis the gift to be simple, 'tis the gift to be free,
'Tis the gift to come down where we ought to be,
And when we find ourselves in the place just right,
'Twill be in the valley of love and delight.
When true simplicity is gain'd,
To bow and to bend we shan't be asham'd,
To turn, turn will be our delight
'Till by turning, turning we come round right."

Original Shaker Hymn

CLUTTERED LIVES

The American dream for too many persons has become a cluttered nightmare. We work too much, sleep too little, commute too far,

Habits of the Heart

exercise rarely, eat badly, and ignore our families. Video games, reality shows on television, and Internet chat rooms replace personal conversations. We long for a life full of habits of the heart and a relationship with God and other people that build us up, yet we cultivate behaviors that do just the opposite. The more complicated life becomes, the less happy we seem to be.

The more cluttered life becomes, it appears that we become less fulfilled. Author Gregg Easterbrook has written:

> Standards of living keep rising, with the typical house now more than twice as large as a generation ago; middle-class income keeps rising . . . ; more Americans graduate from college every year; longevity keeps rising; almost all forms of disease, including most cancers, are in decline; crime has dropped spectacularly; pollution, except for greenhouse gases, is in long-term decline; discrimination is down substantially. Yet despite all these positive indicators, the percentage of Americans who describe themselves as "happy" has not increased since the early 1950s, while incidences of depression keep rising.[1]

Where do we look for relief? In the mid-1990s, a small yet expansively equipped version of a luxury car came onto the North American car market. The average cost of that vehicle exceeded the median family income. In the first television commercials that introduced this car, the background music was the tune from the Shaker hymn that began this chapter. The subtle, ironic message: Spend more money, buy yourself a luxury car, and your life will turn out right. The Shakers would not be pleased by this use of their sacred music, and especially the words that go with the music. Yet, the seductive message that surrounding ourselves with more complex adult toys as the key to happiness is one of the primary messages of contemporary life. As you continue your spiritual quest by traveling some new directions, will you risk setting aside the clutteredness around you and become more like a child, seeing the world in a new way?

What Do I Want to Be When I Grow Up?

WHOSE BIRTHDAY IS IT ANYWAY?

One illustration of cluttered lives is the celebration of Christmas. Christmas, in theory, is a simple time of year. Christmas, simply put, focuses on a poor child born within an animal shelter in a Third-World country. One ideal vision pictures a peaceful family sitting in front of a warm fireplace, drinking hot chocolate, telling family stories, crafting handmade presents, reading the Christmas story, and writing Christmas cards to distant friends and family.

Reality is a little different. We may spend the holidays (which seem very far from "holy days") going to parties we do not wish to attend, spending more money than we have shopping for people who need nothing, eating too much rich food, drinking too much eggnog, and worrying about not sending cards to people we love. No wonder we may be exhausted at the end of the most complicated season of them all. Even Andy, the pastor of a local congregation, sometimes dreads the busyness of Christmas: Sunday school class parties, gifts for co-workers, multiple worship services, special presentations by children, the annual Christmas musical, and the flurry of end-of-the-year record-keeping. Many people thus declare on December 26 not "What a wonderful season!" but "Thank God Christmas is over!"

In our hearts we know better. In most families, the favorite Christmas tree ornaments are not those received from the gift store, but the small, handmade objects created by young children in our families. On Andy's Christmas tree, the most cherished ornaments are the hand-stitched snowflakes woven by his grandmother decades ago. The best meal is not eaten at the corporate Christmas party but at the family breakfast table on Christmas morning. We read the handwritten Christmas card from a friend many more times than the engraved card featuring a posed picture of a beautiful family.

> *"Maybe Christmas," he thought, "doesn't come from a store. Maybe Christmas . . . perhaps . . . means a little bit more!"*
> *The Grinch*

SIMPLICITY AS A HABIT OF THE HEART

In a world cluttered with too much activity, is there an alternative? Jesus Christ suggests that we risk having a childlike approach to life, being more attentive to God and the people around us, enabling simplicity to regain a toehold.

Jesus is not unique in suggesting simplicity. In natural and theoretical sciences, the quest of scientists is to discover the simplest ways that all of nature works together. Albert Einstein, who knew better than most people about the complex forces in nature, declared: "I have deep faith that the principle of the universe will be beautiful and simple."[2]

> *"The call to simplicity and freedom for Christians is the call to move from achievement oriented spirituality to a life centered on a shared vision of relatedness to people and things."*
> *Richard Bower*

As the three of us—Mark, Rob, and Andy—were working on this study, we took a break and drove through the mountains of North Carolina. As we enjoyed the spectacular natural scenery, we also noticed the homes. Some of the mountain homes were built down in the valley, more easily accessible to neighbors and community services. In general, these homes were smaller and more compact. Other homes were built up on the mountaintops. Many of these larger houses included expansive windows and outdoor pools and hot tubs. In these isolated homes, water had to be pumped up the mountain, community resources were more remote, and neighbors were divided by gates and private access roads. We speculated that longtime residents owned the valley homes, and the mountaintop homes were built by persons new to the area. What the mountain natives knew, which the newer residents would learn, was that when the winter storms came, those expensive, mountaintop homes would be cold, isolated, and dangerous. Only the homes in the valley, simpler and more accessible, were truly livable year-round. The message: Less can be more.

JESUS' SIMPLICITY

God risked appearing in the flesh in our world not in the palace of an emperor and clothed in rich clothes. Instead, Jesus Christ was born in an animal stall in an occupied nation among an oppressed people and wrapped in peasant rags (Luke 2). Jesus never purchased a home or piece of property, never owned more clothes than those on his back, walked everywhere, and never established a pension plan. We doubt that he ever went to a Roman spa or took a long vacation at the beach or in the mountains. (He did take that forty-day trip into the desert, but it was no vacation.) Instead, Jesus took time off for quiet prayer. He observed the sabbath and reveled in visiting with his friends. When he entered the capital of Jerusalem at the end of his ministry, Jesus did not arrive on a large white horse in the midst of warriors in battle array. Instead, he rode into Jerusalem on the back of a donkey, surrounded by children and peasants throwing palm branches on the ground (Mark 11:1-11). The king of the universe assumed the status of a peasant. Jesus exemplified simplicity as a habit of his heart.

> *"Christian simplicity is not just a faddish attempt to respond to the ecological holocaust that threatens to engulf us, nor is it born out of a frustration with technocratic obesity.... The witness to simplicity is profoundly rooted in the biblical tradition, and most perfectly exemplified in the life of Jesus Christ."*
> *Richard Foster*

JESUS AND THE CHILDREN

Jesus Christ did not just live a simple life; he suggested that all persons who follow him also adopt a similar habit of the heart. Jesus suggested that when we grow up, we should become like children. He believed that a solution to our cluttered lives is to rediscover the perspective of a child.

Jesus' friends had begun to enjoy the popularity of Jesus' ministry. Large crowds showed up wherever they traveled. The dinner parties were more elaborate and the food better. The financial offerings were probably more generous. Jesus' friends had become like bodyguards and bouncers, monitoring and supervising those persons who could approach Jesus.

One day, some people brought children to see the new teacher so that Jesus could touch the children and bless them. Jesus' friends had no time for children and pushed them away; large contributors and persons with position would come first. When Jesus saw what was happening, he reacted forcefully. Jesus rebuked his friends, welcomed the children to come near, and touched and blessed them. Jesus declared that the children knew more about God than did all the adults in their company.

CHILDLIKE SIMPLICITY

Children have a way of helping us see the world as it really should be. Andy once was at a meeting with community leaders dealing with an issue of racism. The conversation had been intense, and the leaders had divided against one another by the color of their skin. He remembers:

> I was worried whether there ever could be racial harmony. Back in my office, I looked out my window at my congregation's preschool playground sandbox. I saw a pair of two-year-old girls lying on their stomachs in the sand. One child had luminous dark skin and jet-black hair. The other girl was pale white with long, golden hair. The girls had pushed their bodies right together, their heads touching, and their arms linked. Together the girls were drawing designs in the sand with their fingers. Giggling and laughing, they lay together and played in

the sand. They had not yet learned to categorize one another by the color of their skin. Those two children gave me hope that one day racism may be overcome.

"When childhood dies, its corpses are called adults."
Brian Aldiss

Children see through the complexities of life that consume adults. Watch a young toddler when Christmas presents are unwrapped; the child cares more for the wrapping paper and ribbons than for the expensive present inside the box. Children's lives are not so cluttered as are those of adults, at least until the children start watching ads on television. Richard Rohr wrote about children and Jesus this way:

> One of Jesus' favorite visual aids is a child.... He says the only people who can recognize and be ready for what he's talking about are the ones who come with the mind and heart of a child. It's the same reality as the beginner's mind. The older we get, the more we've been betrayed and hurt and disappointed, the more barriers we put up to the beginner's mind. It's so hard to go back, to be vulnerable, to say to your soul, "I don't know anything."[3]

In 1966, Pablo Picasso, the twentieth-century artist, hosted an exhibit of his works in France. Picasso had displayed hundreds of his paintings from the time he was a teenager into his eighties. A woman stopped Picasso and said, "I don't understand. Over there, the beginning pictures—so mature, serious and solemn—then the later ones, so different, so irrepressible. It almost seems as though the dates should be reversed. How do you explain it?" "Easily," replied Picasso, "it takes a long time to become young."[4] As Carlo Caretto wrote:

> The natural progression of life is from childhood to old age. On the contrary, the Kingdom of God within us goes from the age of an old

man to the childhood of the spiritually renewed man. This calls for two yardsticks: during the natural course of life one grows in prudence, wisdom and responsibility; but in spiritual life one grows in childlikeness, simplicity, impulsiveness, joy, clarity and unity of purpose.[5]

Clarence Jordan, a biblical scholar, founded a farming community in south Georgia to create the simpler life suggested by Jesus. From his new environment, Jordan wrote a folksy paraphrase of Jesus' words about how to approach life:

> Therefore, let me tell you something: Don't worry about making a living—what you'll eat, what you'll drink, what you'll wear. Isn't the life of people more than what they eat? Think for a moment about the birds of the sky. They don't plant. They don't harvest. They don't store up in barns. Even so, your spiritual Father cares for them. Really now, aren't you all more precious than birds? Besides, who of you, by fretting and fuming, can make yourself one inch taller? And what's all this big to-do over clothing? Look yonder at that field of flowers, how they're growing. They do no housework and no sewing. But I'm telling you, not even Solomon [the richest King in the Bible] in all his finery was ever dressed up like one of them. Well then, if God so clothes the flowers of the field, which are blooming today and are used for kindling tomorrow, won't God do even more for you, you spiritual runts? So cut out your anxious talk about "what are we gonna eat, and what are we gonna drink, and what are we gonna wear." For the people of the world go tearing around after all these things. Listen, your spiritual Father is quite aware that you've got to have all such stuff. Then set your heart on the God Movement and its kind of life, and all these things will come as a matter of course.
> (Matthew 6:25-33)[6]

SIMPLE LIVES TODAY

Sandi had lived a charmed life. With her college degrees behind her, she climbed the corporate ladder and made good money. Unfortunately, Sandi was miserable. She worked too many hours and wore herself

What Do I Want to Be When I Grow Up?

out. "I got burnt out pretty quickly." Her solution was to leave everything behind and look for a new perspective and a new life. She left Florida and worked to create a simpler world in Wyoming. In the west, Sandi skied, worked with animals, and enjoyed friends and family.

Many people today search for such a simple life. A simple life does not mean selling all our worldly possessions, throwing out the television, disconnecting from the Internet, driving a beat-up old car, buying all our clothes at the Goodwill or Salvation Army store, and reading the newspapers that someone else discards. Some of Andy's friends left behind an increasingly complicated world in the 1960s, moving to a commune out in the country, raising sheep, weaving their own cloth, making their own clothes, and raising their own food. Most of these friends, for better or for worse, have been lured back to our modern world. How can we maintain simplicity without withdrawing from the world?

LENT: A SEASON OF SIMPLICITY

The Christian observance of Lent, the forty-day season that precedes the celebration of Jesus' resurrection at Easter, is one way to counter the complexities that consume our lives. Lent is preceded by a festival called Mardi Gras, when people live excessively; the wild celebrations in New Orleans and other communities have Christian roots! Yet, after the Mardi Gras parties, Lent begins with an odd service on a day called "Ash Wednesday."

On Ash Wednesday people of God gather to sing, pray, and read the Bible. The Ash Wednesday service culminates with an imposition with ashes. The ashes come from burned palm branches creating a deep black powder. As persons kneel, a worship leader marks our foreheads with ashes and says, "From dust you came, to dust you shall return." Being marked with ashes reminds us of our mortality. On a broader level, the Ash Wednesday service calls us to observe a few habits of simplicity throughout Lent.

For the next forty days of Lent (a reminder of Jesus' desert spiritual quest), as a sign to reinforce the imposition of ashes on Ash Wednesday, Christians adopt a simpler life by giving up something cherished. The idea is to catch a vision of and practice a different way of living. Some persons play with the power of self-denial by giving up something they hate—broccoli or brussel sprouts. Other persons go to extremes of inflicting pain upon their bodies. We may sometimes see pictures of individuals in some Christian cultures hitting themselves with whips or nailing one another to crosses. Followers of Jesus do not need to be that extreme. Simply setting aside chocolate or soft drinks or lattes for these forty days can serve as a step toward simplicity. Doing without a Snickers candy bar or a Starbucks espresso for these days reminds us of an uncluttered life. Observing Lent may provide a simple way to move from the clutteredness of life toward the habit of simplicity.

Let the Spirit Guide lead you to simplicity. The observance of the forty days of Lent, and to a lesser extent the four weeks before Christmas called Advent, are occasions to slow down and focus on God. Such observance might include reading the Bible, spending time in prayer, giving money to worthy causes, watching what we eat and drink, and gathering with other Christians at worship.

LIVING WITH CHILDLIKE SIMPLICITY

Mother Teresa of India told a story of how she was taught to see the world through a child's eyes:

> I have learned how to love with great love from a little child in Calcutta. Once, there was no sugar and I do not know how that little Hindu child four years old heard.... He went home and told his parents, "I will not eat sugar for three days: I will give my sugar to Mother Teresa.... After three days they brought him. He was so small, and in his hand there was a little bottle of sugar.... He could scarcely pronounce my name, but yet he gave and the love he put in the giving was beautiful.[7]

What Do I Want to Be When I Grow Up?

How can you be simple, without being simple-minded? The Shakers, a society of folk dedicated to simplicity, followed the Holy Spirit and always encouraged their adherents to be "plain." In their communities, they shared everything with each other. The Shakers suggested that Christians ought to be cautious about what they wear, how they speak, and what they eat in order not to be distracted by the activities of our cluttered world. Deeply infused by the presence of the Guide, Shakers modeled their worship, buildings, clothing, music, and every other aspect of their lives by attentiveness to God. For example, Shaker furniture was simple yet functional and long-lasting. Simple lives led to a more complete love of God and neighbor.

One description of this lifestyle demonstrates a perspective shared by the Shakers:

> The simplicity of lifestyle . . . is not based on forsaking worldly goods and pursuing some vision of a less complex bygone era. It's more like a reliable standard that is always available. . . . Living simply is also not about finding a quiet corner where you can contemplate your life and feel good about yourself. Far from it. It's about giving yourself the freedom to pursue that indestructible impulse to do good in the world, to go toward the best.[8]

"Simplicity, then, is the gift to live a holy life. It is the gift to live in the deeper awareness of connectedness to others and to all creation. It is the gift to travel lightly because accumulation of things, people, and experiences are unnecessary for our joy."   David Crean and Eric and Helen Ebbeson

We, like the Shakers, may be guided by the Holy Spirit to adopt some activities to help us live more in harmony with a simple life. Like a child who sells lemonade to fight hunger in the world, we can take little steps that might add up to profound changes. For the environment, wear clothes until they wear out, turn out the lights when you leave a room, use a hotel towel more than once, recycle newspapers, purchase coffee from earth-friendly farms, and compost yard waste. Helping an elderly person across a street, reading a story to a child, purchasing a meal for a street person, saying please and thank you, letting a car enter a line of traffic, listening to an older relative tell a family story, and helping a neighbor on a project each have the potential to change how we love God and others.

> *"Unless you are simple, you cannot recognize God, the Simple One."* — Bengali Song

The examples of simple living may encompass every area of our lives. We may limit the time we watch television or invite a friend out to eat a meal or share a cup of coffee or tea. We may turn off the radio and go for a walk outdoors. Instead of watching the latest movie, visit the library and read a book. Even better, start a book club. Take a break one day every week or play a board game with a child. Plant a garden, cultivate the plants, eliminate the weeds, and enjoy the fruits of your labor. Take a nap. Say no. Walk to work or ride public transportation. And, especially at Christmas, cultivate only the habits you wish to observe. Slowly, steadily, these habits will simplify our lives.

> *"Our life is frittered away by detail. Simplicity, simplicity, simplicity! I say, let your affairs be two or three and not a hundred or a thousand."* — Henry David Thoreau

PEELING AWAY

In the movie *Shrek*, the large, green, ugly ogre Shrek tried to explain to his donkey friend that ogres are more complex than most people realize. As Shrek said, "Ogres are like onions. We have layers." The donkey never understood Shrek's point, but Shrek spoke the truth. Everyone has layers; and sometimes, to have new insight

What Do I Want to Be When I Grow Up?

into our spiritual quest, we need to allow the Guide to peel away some of those layers.

Roger was a man who learned how to be more like a child. Growing up in a home with no religious training, he ridiculed Christians as a young adult. Roger met a few devout Christians and even occasionally attended worship, but Christianity was not a part of his life. Then, with his career as a lawyer, his marriage, and the birth of children, Roger decided to participate in the life of an Episcopal congregation. One morning, his pastor preached about becoming a child of God. Roger experienced "this longing, just a longing in my heart, and a sadness because of a realization that I did not have the relationship that he was talking about." Soon, Roger had a transforming experience: "I had a vision of the layers of my soul being peeled away, like an onion. Layer after layer after layer, peeling away. And I was aware that my whole emotional and intellectual façade was unraveling, until it was smaller and smaller. It was down to the size of a pea."[9] When Roger risked letting his life grow smaller, he could then really begin to grow. By peeling away the layers of our complicated lives, we may discover who we really are. Only by beginning to grow as a child of God can we become a mature follower of Jesus Christ.

> *"Simplicity, like all virtues, is valuable because it is useful. I have come to understand that making life simpler does for our minds what getting in shape does for our bodies. It makes us feel more in control, more centered, more effective. . . . I have found that simplicity is an indispensable ally in giving ordinary life extraordinary meaning."*   Robert Smith

Consider the children. Consider the birds of the air and the flowers in the field. Their simple trust in God gives them all they need. Maybe you too can become like them, a simple person who simply follows Jesus Christ.

1. From *The Charlotte Observer* (February 27, 2004); page 11A.
2. From *home.att.net/~quotesabout/alberteinstein.html*
3. From *Everything Belongs* (The Crossroad Publishing Company, 1999) in *A Guide to Prayer for All Who Seek God,* by Rueben Job and Norman Shawchuck (Upper Room Books, 2003); page 206.
4. From *Alive in Christ,* by Maxie Dunnam (Abingdon Press, 1982) in *A Guide to Prayer for All Who Seek God,* by Rueben Job and Norman Shawchuck; page 251.
5. From *The Desert Journal: A Diary 1954–55* (HarperCollins, 1991) in *A Guide to Prayer for All Who Seek God,* by Rueben Job and Norman Shawchuck; page 38.
6. From *The Cotton Patch Version of Matthew and John,* by Clarence Jordan (Association Press, 1970); excerpts, pages 27–28. Edited for inclusive language.
7. From *My Life for the Poor: Mother Teresa's Life and Work in Her Own Words,* by Jose Luis Gonzalez-Balado and Janet N. Playfoot (HarperCollins, 1985) in *A Guide to Prayer for All Who Seek God,* by Rueben Job and Norman Shawchuck; pages 53–54.
8. From *A Quaker Book of Wisdom,* by Robert Smith (Eagle Brook, 1998); pages 50–51.
9. From *Finding Faith,* by Sharon Gallagher (Page Mill Press, 2001); pages 113–14.

Six: How Do I Keep My Possessions From Possessing Me?

The Spiritual Habit of Giving

"To have what we want is riches, but to be able to do without is power."   Gordon MacDonald

As Jesus looked up, he saw the rich putting their gifts into the temple [in Jerusalem] treasury. [Jesus] also saw a poor widow put in two very small copper coins. "Truly I tell you," he said, "this poor widow has put in more than all the others. All these people gave their gifts out of their wealth; but she out of her poverty put in all she had to live on."   (Luke 21:1-4)

In the book *Tuesdays with Morrie,* a college professor dying with ALS (Amyotrophic Lateral Sclerosis or "Lou Gehrig's Disease") shared the wisdom of his experience with a former student named Mitch. One day, Morrie reflected on possessions:

> We've got a form of brainwashing going on in our country.... They repeat something over and over.... Owning things is good. More money is good. More property is good. More commercialism is good. More is good. We repeat it—and have it repeated to us—over and over until nobody bothers to even think otherwise.... You know how I always interpret that? These were people so hungry for love that they were accepting substitutes. They were embracing material things and expecting a hug back. But it never works. You can't substitute material things for love."[1]

Morrie was right. All of us are living in a culture that tries to feed our spiritual hunger with material possessions. Advertisements tempt us with the latest models and newest products. Television shows document every detail of the spending habits of wealthy celebrities. Glossy magazines take us into the lavish homes of people who have "made it." Every day, we are bombarded with the promise that true contentment can be found through the things we possess. The root of our materialistic obsessions, however, is not social, psychological, or even economic. The problem with possessions is spiritual. We cannot be both a spiritual inquirer and an obsessive material acquirer. To develop a heart-healthy relationship with our possessions, to go deeper in our relationship with Jesus Christ, the Spirit must enable us to become dis-possessed.

THE PURSUIT OF POSSESSIONS

"People spend their lives wanting things they shouldn't. The world confuses them into taking their love and aiming it where it doesn't belong.... It is better to love something that can love you back."

Ian Caldwell & Dustin Thomason

Becoming dis-possessed is not easy. Consumerism has become the dominant ethos of American life. Shopping is a national pastime. In 1986, the United States of America had more high schools than shopping centers; today, the country has twice as many shopping centers as high schools.[2] In North Carolina, a giant mega-mall is the number-one tourist attraction, a modern cathedral to the religion of acquisitiveness. And, like all religions, consumerism has its own vision of the good life: "Buy, display, discard." Many people have become like the misguided character in Kurt Vonnegut's novel, *Slaughterhouse Five,* who "was trying to construct a life that made sense from things she found in gift shops."[3]

How Do I Keep My Possessions From Possessing Me?

Jesus Christ understood this habit of acquisitiveness and its potential to hurt people in their spiritual quests. He once spoke with his followers this way:

"Watch out! Be on your guard against all kinds of greed; life doesn't consist in an abundance of possessions."

Then Jesus told the crowd of inquirers this parable: "The fields of a certain rich man yielded an abundant harvest. The rich man thought to himself, 'What shall I do? I have no place to store my crops.'

"Then the rich man said, 'This is what I'll do. I'll tear down my barns and build bigger barns, and there I will store my surplus grain. And I'll say to myself, "You have plenty of grain laid up for many years. Take life easy; eat, drink, and be merry.' "

"But God said to the rich man, 'You fool! This very night I will demand your life from you. Then who will get what you have prepared for yourself?' "

Jesus then ended: "This is how it will be with those people who store up things for themselves but are not rich toward God."

(Luke 12:15-21, author's translation)

In this culture of acquisitiveness, many people believe that "eat, drink, and be merry, for tomorrow you may die" is a positive style of life; but this approach is the opposite of what Jesus suggested. A life that celebrates possessions alone and their immediate enjoyment never makes sense. Time spent roaming the mall keeps us from connecting with people we love. Families go to war over inheritances. Eating out at costly restaurants replaces cooking soul food at home. Far too many people take on foolish levels of debt, merely renting lifestyles they cannot afford. American households today average thousands of dollars in high-interest credit card debt.

In the unchecked pursuit of possessions, we lose more than we gain. We may feel bloated and sluggish, tense and anxious. We may suffer through a burned-out career, ruined relationships, and a stressed-out body all in the pursuit of possessions. Syndicated columnist Ellen Goodman was heard saying: "Normal is getting dressed in clothes that you buy for work, driving through traffic in a car that you are still paying for, in order to get to a job that you need so you can pay for the clothes, car, and the house that you leave empty all day in order to afford to live in it."[4]

"It is better to have fewer wants than to have larger resources."
Saint Augustine

On a collective level, human beings unintentionally exploit the possessions that belong to the whole planet. The seas are over-fished as we take popular sea creatures and throw away the rest of the catch as waste. Rainforests and rare species disappear to reduce the price of a morning cup of coffee served on tables made of rare woods. Some persons in North American society have forgotten the energy crises of the recent past and still purchase vehicles that burn too much gas. We drill oil from the earth and create greenhouse gases that overwhelm our atmosphere. We let food rot in the fields, yet allow much of humanity to go hungry. Humans now consume the same amount of fresh water on golf courses as would be needed to provide every person in the world eight glasses of water a day. We have become addicted to material consumption, apparently believing that when God said, "Be fruitful and multiply; and have dominion . . . over every living thing that moves upon the earth (Genesis 1:28)," we were being given permission to abuse planet Earth.

"We are living in a world that rejects love and that affirms selfishness as the ultimate value. The pressure from society is constantly insinuating itself through our upbringing, education, and culture. Society as a whole is saturated with the non-God."
Thomas Keating

How Do I Keep My Possessions From Possessing Me?

The ancient Greek author Aesop once wrote a fable about the destructive quality of seeking more possessions. In "The Dog and His Shadow," a dog receives a fine, meaty bone. On the way home, with the bone firmly between his teeth, the dog crosses a bridge over a small, still pond. When the dog looks down into the water, he sees his own reflection magnified. Thinking that the other dog has a larger bone, the dog decides to take the new, larger bone by force. He leans over the bridge and barks at his own reflection. And as the dog barks, the bone between his teeth falls into the water and is lost. Aesop knew we all want more than what we have, yet often in the process lose what we have.

THE BIGGEST LOSS

The biggest loss caused by all this consumerism and focus on possessions is spiritual. Newspaper columnist John Atcheson put it this way: "When [creating wealth] becomes an end in itself, when it is not informed by deeper values, it simply expands our waistlines and shrinks our souls."[5] Unbridled consumption leads to feelings of emptiness and restlessness. When we derive our identity from the things we possess—cars, clothes, credit cards, electronic devices, and vacations—we confuse the trappings of the good life with life itself. As the distinction between our stuff and ourselves becomes blurred, we often feel incomplete and anxious.

When newswoman Barbara Walters once interviewed billionaire Ted Turner, she recounted many of Turner's most prized possessions at the time: a baseball team, television networks, yachts, ranches, and tremendous bank accounts. Just before the interview ended, Walters asked, "What does it feel like to be so wealthy?" Turner responded, "It's like a paper bag. Everyone sees the bag. Everyone wants it. Once you get the bag, you discover that the bag is empty." In an unscripted moment, Turner revealed that his own pursuit of possessions did not leave him fulfilled but empty.[6]

Turner had discovered something as old as the human race. An Old Testament songwriter described what happens to people when possessions are their only goal:

> The idols of the world are silver and gold,
>   the work of human hands.
> These idols have mouths, but they do not speak;
>   they have eyes, but they do not see;
> they have ears, but they do not hear,
>   and there is no breath in their mouths.
> Those people who make these idols,
> and all who trust their own idols,
> shall become like these idols.
>   (Psalm 135:15-18, author's translation)

Emptiness leads to restlessness. In a magazine advertisement for a luxury car, two adults are featured in the ad with their backs turned. The copy reads: "Little Kids Are Selfish. Impulsive. They Don't Make Rational Decisions. When They See Something They Want, They Want It Now. Little Kids Have a Lot of Fun. Hmmmm."[7] This restlessness is what an early Christian named Augustine meant when he said that our hearts are "forever restless until they rest in God."[8]

The message of consumerism is: "Whatever I want, I want it now!" The problem with acquisitiveness is that wants, by definition, are impossible to satisfy. We may placate our wants for a while, but our wants always re-emerge wanting something else, craving a newer, improved version of what we have already got. Because there will always be something else out there that we do not possess, we may discover that we live in a state of perpetual restlessness. We become consumed by the awareness that something is missing from our lives, but we keep searching in places that offer no real promise of fulfillment.

How Do I Keep My Possessions From Possessing Me?

"The archetypal idea of the consumer society that... 'You are the most important thing on earth.'... There's no message possible that runs more nearly counter to the message of Jesus."

Michael Schut

A WIDOW'S STORY

Is there an alternative? Is it possible to find relief from our possessions? As we journey on our spiritual quest, as we travel in different directions, can the Guide help our hearts discover something spiritual as the source of fullness and satisfaction?

Jesus believed that we can break the power of our possessions over us. We can risk loving God and our neighbors in ways that break our addiction to our possessions. Jesus proved that such a virtue was possible by pointing out to his followers a woman whose possessions did not overwhelm her.

One day, while Jesus and his friends were in the courtyard of the Temple, the main religious edifice in Jerusalem, they observed people placing their financial gifts in a large collection bowl. This action resembles people putting their money into a Salvation Army kettle before Christmas. In those days before paper money, the sound of the metal coins would declare to everyone who gave what. Large, heavy coins sounded loudly throughout the courtyard. In the hearing of Jesus and his followers, some rich persons quite obviously offered a large number of heavy coins.

Then a widow arrived. How would Jesus know that she was a widow? She probably arrived unaccompanied by a man. Because she was a widow, this woman was also poor. In that culture and time, widows were wards of their husband's families; widows were among the poorest people in the land. This woman contributed just two small coins into the common pot: clink, clink. Jesus stated, "This poor widow has put in more than all the others. All these people gave their gifts out of their wealth; but she out of her poverty put in all she had to live on" (Luke 21:3-4).

"The abundant life is characterized by freedom: freedom to define our security and well-being in terms of relationship with God rather than the amount of stuff we've accumulated."
Michael Schut

How could two small coins outweigh significantly larger gifts? The religious treasurers probably appreciated more the gifts of large contributors. For Jesus, the issue was not how much the woman contributed, but rather how much she gave up with her offering. The answer: She willingly gave up all her financial possessions. What did she have left after her offering? Absolutely nothing. This woman understood that she was completely dependent on God for everything. She dropped her entire savings into the pot but kept intact her dependence upon God. Her habit of the heart becomes a model for all persons who follow Jesus.

GIVING AS A HABIT OF THE HEART

"Let us try to teach generosity and altruism, because we are born selfish. . . . We have the power to defy the selfish genes of our birth. . . . We, alone on earth, can rebel against the tyranny of the selfish replicators."
Richard Dawkins

The alternative to acquisitiveness is generosity. The deepest kind of happiness comes from giving, knowing that we are offering our possessions to help other people. When we become dis-possessed, when we give a portion of our possessions away, we can feel in our heart that our life makes a difference.

Oseola McCarty never made much money. When she was in the sixth grade, her childless aunt became sick, and McCarty left school to care for her. She was never able to return to school. For more than seventy-five years, McCarty earned what she could washing and ironing other people's clothes in her modest frame home in Hattiesburg, Mississippi. She was paid very little, but each week she

How Do I Keep My Possessions From Possessing Me?

took a small part of what she earned and deposited it in the bank. McCarty observed this habit of the heart for decades. She never took any money out and never thought too much about it. One day, when she was eighty-seven years old, McCarty's bank teller informed her, "Oseola, do you know you have accumulated quite a bit of money over the years? In fact, you now have more than $250,000." Another bank employee helped McCarty visualize how much money this was. The employee put ten dimes on the counter and asked, "If these dimes represented your money, and each one was worth $25,000, what would you like to do with those dimes?"

McCarty pondered the question deeply. She said, "I will give one dime to my church, three dimes to my nieces and nephews because they need help and have been so good to me, and the rest of the dimes I would like to use to set up a college fund for African-American students who still dare to dream." This is exactly what McCarty did; she established a scholarship fund at the University of Southern Mississippi. The media picked up her story. The press told about her remarkable ability to save from the smallest of resources and her amazing generosity. She wound up meeting prime ministers and presidents. McCarty received an honorary doctorate from Harvard University. Ted Turner—the mogul who had expressed his own misgivings about possessions to Barbara Walters—also heard this story. Turner said, "If Oseola can give away her life savings, then I guess I could give away a billion dollars." And so Turner made an unprecedented donation in that amount to the United Nations.[9]

GENEROSITY AS A SIGN OF SPIRITUALITY

Simplicity, the subject of the previous chapter, involves getting rid of the clutteredness in our lives. But simplicity by itself is not enough.

Habits of the Heart

"Simplicity is not so much about what we own, but about what owns us. If we need lots of possessions to maintain our self-esteem and create our self-image and to look good to our neighbors, then we have forgotten or neglected that which is real and inward."
Christin Hadley Snyder

An additional habit of the heart is using what we possess, whether little or much, for the sake of God and our neighbors. To risk using our possessions for the greater good, releasing our possessions for the benefit of God and our neighbors, is a positive and proactive habit of the heart. This habit is called generosity.

The spiritual habit of generosity begins with a fundamental principle of the Christian life: We own nothing. Everything we possess belongs not to us but to God. Christians believe that God created everything: "In the beginning . . . God created the heavens and the earth" (Genesis 1:1). And Christians believe that God still owns everything that God created: "The earth is the LORD'S and all that is in it" (Psalm 24:1). God placed us in the midst of a wonderful creation and gave us life, time, talents, companions, and everything else we have. We, therefore, are simply the temporary holder of a few of God's possessions.

"You possess only whatever will not be lost in a shipwreck."
Al-Ghazali

Knowing that God is the ultimate owner of every single thing, what then is our role in God's creation? Our spiritual habit is to make a grateful, generous response to God's many gifts.

STEWARDS

The biblical word Christians use for taking responsibility for possessions is *steward*. The word comes from the Greek *oikonomia,* meaning "a person who manages the household affairs for a wealthy person."

How Do I Keep My Possessions From Possessing Me?

Native Americans in the United States understand this biblical perspective well. Tradition tells us that the indigenous peoples of North America were amused at the Europeans' desire to own land in the New World. Native Americans were willing to accept payment by the Europeans for the land, knowing full well that only the Creator truly owned it.

Tom Roughface, from the Ponca Tribe in Oklahoma, expressed this biblical perspective. Tom had long been an active leader of United Methodist Native Americans. Upon his death in 2003, his family sponsored a traditional "Giveaway" gathering for all his friends at the Ponca Tribal Center. As hundreds of people gathered, Tom's family began to distribute gifts: to a family who was hungry, a basket of food; to a family who lost a home through fire, a box of supplies; and to everyone there, at least a blanket or a shawl. Instead of receiving gestures of support from the community, Tom's family offered gifts of love. As Tom's granddaughter described the event, "We believe that you can accept death better by giving than by getting." This "Giveaway" tradition from a Native American nation demonstrates clearly a Christian perspective about our possessions.[10]

"A good chief gives, he does not take."   Mohawk Proverb

In Christianity, stewards are the persons who manage the possessions of God. We are the stewards of our time, talents, and possessions but certainly not the rightful owner. During the second century after Jesus Christ, an observer wrote to the Roman Emperor Hadrian about Christians and focused on their loving stewardship:

> "They love one another. They never fail to help widows; they save orphans from those who would hurt them. If they have something, they give freely to the one who has nothing; if they see a stranger, they take the stranger home. . . . They don't consider themselves brothers and sisters in the usual sense, but brothers and sisters instead through the Spirit, in God."

Christians believe that it is God's nature to give. God gave us life. God gave us the fellowship of other people. God gave us food, shelter, and clothing. God gave us our talents and skills and the ability to earn a living. God even gave us God's most precious possession: "For God so loved the world that God gave the only Son" (John 3:16, author's translation). Our habit of being a good steward is our response to God's love for us. We imitate God's giving. The issue is not how much we possess but what we do with what we manage for God.

JESUS AND MONEY

Jesus spoke about money more than nearly any other subject. He was rather clear about his expectations of how his followers must act. They were to use their financial resources to feed the hungry, give water to the thirsty, welcome the stranger, and clothe the naked (Matthew 25). Jesus did not say that it is wrong to make money. He mingled freely with both the poor and the rich. He sometimes ate with wealthy people (Luke 7:36; 11:37); and many of his closest followers, such as Joseph of Arimethea and Nicodemus, were persons of considerable wealth (Matthew 27:57; John 19:39).

Yet, Jesus found that excessive possessions could be an obstacle to spiritual growth. He once said, "It is easier for a camel to go through the eye of a needle than for the rich to enter the kingdom of God" (Matthew 19:24). Using this hyperbole, Jesus overturned a prevailing assumption of his day. Wealth was seen as God's reward for living a righteous life; anyone who had money was understood to be favored in God's eyes. The opposite was also believed; anyone who was poor was assumed to be unrighteous. Jesus, in overturning this assumption, wanted to make clear that God loved poor people, and that riches could easily become an obstacle to finding the abundant life God longs for us to experience.

Jesus said, "Do not store up for yourselves treasures on earth, where moth and rust destroy, and where thieves break in and steal.

How Do I Keep My Possessions From Possessing Me?

But store up for yourselves treasures in heaven, where moth and rust do not destroy, and where thieves do not break in and steal. For where your treasure is, there your heart will be also" (Matthew 6:19-21). Jesus did not promise a one-to-one correspondence between faithful giving and receiving; a dollar given does not guarantee a dollar back from God. Yet, God does provide "our daily bread" (Luke 11:3); and Jesus said, "Give, and it will be given to you" (Luke 6:38). Ultimately, stewardship is a habit of the heart, a grateful response to all we have received from God, indicating that we live our lives in partnership with God.

HOW MUCH MONEY AM I TO GIVE?

"If money determines what we do or do not do, then money is our boss. If God determines what we do or do not do, then God is our boss."
Richard J. Foster

For many people, their most prized possession is their money. They guard it more zealously than any other object. Regarding money, therefore, how do we become dis-possessed? How much money are we supposed to give?

There are at least two major traditions about the giving of money. The traditional model is tithing, giving ten percent of our income to God through a religious community or congregation (Numbers 18:25). Many Christians have tithed and continue to tithe. Jesus never rejected the tithe as a model of giving. The difficulty is that tithing seems rather legalistic. Some persons debate whether the ten percent should be based on net income, gross income, or net worth. Other people suggest that because so many governmental social programs now care for the poor, the tithe should be reduced to five percent. This debate seems to have little to do with generosity.

Another biblical model is proportional giving. Proportional giving means that we give to God a set portion of our money. The Old

Testament also suggests this model: "All shall give as they are able, according to the blessing . . . that God has given to you" (Deuteronomy 16:17, author's translation). Proportional giving suggests that some persons, such as people with serious health crises or critical needs at home, give a smaller percentage of their income. On the other side, some persons, such as people with higher disposable incomes or fewer needs at home, should give a larger percentage of their income. The strange thing, however, is that studies show that persons with smaller incomes give away a higher percentage of their money than do persons with higher incomes. This statistic simply demonstrates the pervasive and destructive power of money; the more comfortable we become the less we remember our need to be a good steward.

Let us be clear. There is no one absolute biblical model for giving of our money. There is no divine 1040 Form (or 1040A!) with thousands of pages of instructions and a heavenly Internal Revenue Service checking our statement. There is no group of angels with green eyeshades in heaven auditing our returns. Our giving is a private agreement between us and God. What is required is intentionality. What do you choose to give?

> *"A confrontation with Jesus is . . . not unlike sifting through the ashes after a fire has destroyed our home and the possessions of a lifetime. In that aftermath we slowly relearn what we actually keep and what we value most."*   Donald J. Shelby

To whom should we give our money? Some Christians believe that we should give every penny we contribute to God through the church. Yet, in every community there are multiple opportunities to give: the Salvation Army, the street person on the corner, the homeless shelter, the food pantry, the youth club, the political party, the school emergency fund, the missionary overseas or in an impoverished corner of our nation, national and international emergencies—

the list goes on and on. Again, the issue is not how much or to whom we give, but with what foresight and forethought, as a habit of the heart.

MODELS OF STEWARDS

"When God breaks in... a new generosity emerges, one that is outgoing, joyous, spontaneous and free.... A new stewardship unfolds, a stewardship that cares deeply for all of God's created order, including the earth and its fullness—people, animals and things."   Edward J. Farrell

One style of living as a steward comes from a saint who lived eight hundred years ago, Francis of Assisi. His father was a wealthy cloth merchant who indulged his son's every whim. Francis grew up to love fine clothes and great parties. He joined the army and toured Italy. Francis was like a fraternity brother at a major party college with a rich daddy and a Porsche. He partied hard, had lots of girlfriends, and cared nothing for Jesus.

By age twenty-three, however, Francis began to have dreams, dreams that made him question the direction of his life. Francis began a quest to explore a different set of priorities. He gave money to lepers, exchanged clothes with a tattered wanderer, and fasted with the poor. One day, he walked into his father's shop, loaded one of his father's horses with a pile of colored drapery, and then sold the cloth and the horse to raise money for his local congregation. When Francis's father heard what his son had done, he believed that Francis had gone mad. His father dragged Francis home, beat him, disinherited him, and locked him in a closet. When Francis came out of this closet, he stripped himself of all his clothes and, inspired by the Holy Spirit, said something like this to his father: "Until now, I called you my father; from now on, I will only serve our Father/God who is in heaven."

Although some people believe poverty to be a threat or handicap, Francis found poverty to be a blessing. Francis had found the meaning of his life. He gave away all his possessions, put on a coarse brown tunic (the clothing of a peasant), tied a rope around his waist, and walked barefooted. He became the most passionate lover of poverty our world has ever seen. Francis called his new first love "Lady Poverty." Some historians say that Francis saved Christianity in Europe, reminding people that Christianity is not for the wealthy and powerful but for people who give everything to God. Today, we call Francis a saint. By focusing on Jesus and rejecting all else, Francis discovered a place in heaven.

Not every saint is famous. Stewardship indicates that we live our lives in a grateful partnership with God. Andy tells the story of Edith, a member of his first congregation.

> Edith was born in a family of tenant farmers and worked at a textile mill all her life. She never owned a car. At her retirement, Edith's wealth consisted of a four-room mill home, plus her Social Security check. Each month when she received her check, Edith cashed it and walked from store to store paying her bills. Each month, Edith also gave me ten percent ($40) of her Social Security check ($400) in cash to place in the offering plate at worship. One month, I took Edith's gift back to her, saying, "Edith, you need this money more than our congregation." Edith then told me, "If you won't take the cash, I'll just send it straight to the church treasurer." She continued, "I'm not giving this money for our church, or for you, or for me, but for God. It's my way of saying thank you to God. Don't take away my chance to give." I was wrong; Edith was right.

"Give me neither poverty or riches; let me be fed with the food that is needful for me."

(Proverbs 30:8, author's translation)

How Do I Keep My Possessions From Possessing Me?

KEEP YOUR FOCUS

Like the saints, keep your eyes on God. Let the Holy Spirit focus your attention on a profound and passionate love of God. That focus will help you discover the pathway to God that does not go through your possessions. Instead of admiring the lifestyles of the rich and famous, risk looking at people who have the spiritual habit of giving. Remember the opening observation by Morrie to Mitch about people substituting material possessions for love. Morrie's conversation with Mitch ended this way: "Remember what I said about finding a meaningful life.... Devote yourself to loving others, devote yourself to your community around you, and devote yourself to creating something that gives you purpose and meaning."[12]

---

1. From *Tuesdays with Morrie,* by Mitch Albom (Doubleday, 1997); pages 124–25.
2. From *Affluenza: The All-Consuming Epidemic,* by Thomas H. Naylor (Berrett-Koehler, 2001); pages 13–14.
3. From *Slaughterhouse Five,* by Kurt Vonnegut (Dell, 1969).
4. Heard. No source.
5. From John Atchenson, *The Baltimore Sun* in *The Charlotte Observer* (11 April 2004); page E-1.
6. From *Running on Empty: Contemplative Spirituality for Overachievers,* by Fil Anderson (Waterbrook, 2004); pages 27–28.
7. From *Who Are We? Critical Reflections and Hopeful Possibilities,* by Jean Bethke Elshtain (Eerdmans, 2000); pages 39–40.
8. From *The Confessions of St. Augustine,* by Augustine, translated by E. B. Pusey (E.P. Dutton, 1951); page 1.
9. From *Second Innocence: Rediscovering Joy and Wonder,* by John Izzo (Berrett-Koehler, 2004); pages 164–65.
10. Based on conversations between Andy and persons in attendance at Tom Roughface's funeral.
11. From *God's Treasury of Virtues* (Honor Books, 1995); page 43. Edited for inclusive language.
12. From *Tuesdays with Morrie,* by Mitch Albom; page 127.

Seven:
How Do I Get Ahead?

The Spiritual Habit of Serving

"I don't know what your destiny will be, but one thing I know: The only ones among you who will be really happy are those who have sought and found a way to serve." Albert Schweitzer

It was just before the Passover Festival [the annual Jewish celebration of their liberation from slavery in Egypt]....

The evening meal was in progress.... [Jesus] got up from the meal, took off his outer clothing, and wrapped a towel around his waist. After that, [Jesus] poured water into a basin and began to wash his disciples' feet, drying them with the towel that was wrapped around him....

When he had finished washing their feet, [Jesus] put on his clothes and returned to his place. "Do you understand what I have done for you?" he asked them. "You call me 'Teacher' and 'Lord,' and rightly so, for that is what I am. Now that I, your Lord and Teacher, have washed your feet, you also should wash one another's feet. I have set you an example that you should do as I have done for you. Very truly I tell you, servants are not greater than their master, nor are messengers greater than the one who sent them. Now that you know these things, you will be blessed if you do them." (John 13:1-17)

A SERVICE ECONOMY

We live within a service economy. No longer is manufacturing the base of our economic system, but people offering personal services to one another. From computer consultants to waiters, from financial analysts to housecleaners, from political consultants to entertainers to store clerks, a majority of people make their living by providing personal assistance to other people. The mantras of this society include: "May I help you?" "How may I serve you?" "Would you like anything else?" "The customer is always right!" It seems as if everyone has become everyone else's genie in a bottle: "Your wish is my command."

Strangely, however, in this environment we have all been taught to expect service rather than to provide service. Rather than giving thanks for simple gestures of help, we believe we are entitled to superior care. We may sometimes serve another person primarily so that the other will serve us; I will help you if you will help me. In this service economy, everyone has forgotten how to serve! A genuine offer of care and help remains unexpected. This service economy, oddly, has made the idea of Christian service as a habit of the heart seem even stranger.

A CULTURE OF ENTITLEMENT

Remember James and John from the first chapter, those two enthusiastic fishermen who climbed out of the boat and followed Jesus? If we find their willingness to risk intimidating, then the following story should make us feel better. One day their mother came to Jesus and asked a question that pleasantly embarrassed James and John. Their mother requested that her two boys be placed on the right and left side of Jesus, the two positions of greatest prestige and honor. Their mother longed to see her boys succeed in God's upcoming reign and requested a fancy title and a corner office for her two little angels (Matthew 20:17-28).

Hang out with a group of people long enough and sooner or later folks will start trying to get ahead of one another. This is the culture of entitlement. We have money and we expect to make more money. We have things and expect to possess more things. We hang out with the right people and we expect respect. We are born into the right family and we expect other right families to welcome us.

The actress Meryl Streep, once giving a university commencement address, told the graduating class that when they got out into the real world, life would not be like college. "It will instead, be more like high school."[1] In high school, everyone wants to be at the top of the pyramid of power, and Streep believed that the rest of life follows this model. Streep has a point, and one wonders where it will all end. Will we one day be jockeying for a spot at the "cool table" in the nursing home cafeteria?

MOVING TO THE FRONT OF THE LINE

"Goodness is something so simple; always live for others, never to seek one's own advantage." Dag Hammarskjöld

Ironically, a dogged pursuit of being served by everyone, a life of entitlement, can often keep us from one of life's greatest gifts—a spiritual life. Shortly before he died of a brain tumor, Lee Atwater, a well-known political strategist, looked back on his own pursuit with resignation: "The 1980s were about acquiring—acquiring wealth, power, prestige. I know; I acquired more wealth, power, and prestige than most. But you can acquire all you want and still feel empty." We may assume that those people who "get ahead" in the world—persons with the most prestige, power and possessions—are the most fulfilled. Atwater's words tell us otherwise. For the terminally-ill Atwater and many other people, a misguided pursuit of being served is a kind of cancer, revealing "a spiritual vacuum at the heart of American society, a tumor of the soul."[2]

SERVICE AS A HABIT OF THE HEART

Jesus Christ offered a different path. He told his friends that they would find authentic life not by filling themselves with prestige and power but by emptying themselves in service: "Very truly I tell you, unless a kernel of wheat falls to the ground and dies, it remains only a single seed. But if it dies, it produces many seeds. Those who love their life will lose it, while those who hate their life in this world will keep it for eternal life" (John 12:24-25). When Jesus refers to "life in this world," he is speaking of life as it usually is, a selfish pursuit of self-fulfillment and the dream of being served by everyone. "Eternal life" is Jesus' vision for a true spiritual life, a deep connection with God that lasts throughout our earthly days and continues forever in the presence of God.

Jesus' path to spiritual life reverses the typical expectations of secular society. How can emptying ourselves bring true happiness? There are easy, everyday answers that prove Jesus' point. Ask a pregnant woman; the travails of giving birth are quickly overcome by the gift of new life. Ask someone who has lost weight; the joy of good health far outweighs the missed desserts. Perhaps we can catch Jesus' vision by comparing Atwater's description of the 1980s—often remembered as the "me-decade"—with a different time in United States history. Some people have described the 1930s—the decade of the Great Depression—as the happiest time of their lives. How could that be? A member of Mark's congregation explained it this way:

> I guess it was because we weren't worried about getting ahead. You couldn't get ahead no matter how hard you tried so you just didn't worry about it. But folks pulled together. If a family didn't have enough to eat, somebody would leave a basket of food on their porch. You knew it could just as easily be you. The funny thing was when times got better it wasn't the same. We focused on buying houses, working all the time. We forgot each other. We lost something after that time.

God created us to experience a deep contentment in this life and the next. Ideally, in our quest the Holy Spirit will ultimately lead us to an intimate relationship with God. Yet, this spiritual life requires going beyond our desire to get ahead or be served. We will have to be caught up in the Spirit serving a cause that is greater than ourselves. The mystery of service reveals that nothing has the capacity to bring us so much joy as genuine acts of selfless service.

"I slept and dreamed that life was joy. I awoke and saw that life was service. I served and found service was joy."
Butch Owen

THE ETERNAL SERVANT

"We have seen what Jesus was like. If we wish now to treat Jesus as our God, we would have to conclude that our God does not want to be served by us, God wants to serve."
Albert Nolan

The Gospels make clear that Jesus viewed himself not as a king, emperor, or ruler but as a servant. Jesus once said, "[I] did not come to be served, but to serve" (Mark 10:45). His life demonstrated this truth. Jesus was born in the starkest of simplicity and served by teaching, healing, and feeding the hungry. Jesus exhibited a passionate enthusiasm for the forgotten people of his day: women, children, the poor, and the dying. Because the servant Jesus is the clearest indication of God, then, as implausible as it sounds, God, the Supreme Ruler, is also the Eternal Servant.

Christians recount Jesus Christ's deep desire for service in Philippians 2:6-11. In the words of possibly the first Christian hymn, the poet says that all followers of Jesus Christ should have the same attitude as Christ who, "being in very nature God, / did not consider equality with God something to be used to his own advantage; / rather he made himself nothing / by taking the very nature of a servant" (Philippians 2:6-7). This hymn declared that, although being God himself, Jesus chose to live his earthly life as a servant. In other words, Jesus did not become a servant in spite of his unique connection to God but because of it. Precisely because Jesus Christ was God, he emptied himself for other people. When Jesus came in the form of a servant, he revealed who God really was and is.

> *"It seemed, so great my happiness*
> *That I was blessed and could bless."*
>
> W. B. Yeats

WASHING FEET

Jesus told the women and men who followed him in many different ways that the foolish attitude of jockeying for position would only make them miserable. But these followers could never quite grasp this crucial point. So on the evening before his death, Jesus decided that the time had come to demonstrate a way of living that leads to real, lasting joy. Jesus took off his cloak and wrapped it around his waist. He picked up a basin of water and a towel. Then Jesus Christ began to perform the most menial of tasks, a duty fit only for a lowly servant. In one of the most powerful images of the Bible, the Son of God on his hands and knees humbly washed the dust and grime off the feet of people too concerned about their pecking order ever to do such a thing for one another. When Jesus had finished, he said, "If you make this act a metaphor for your life, if you seek to serve rather than to be served, you will find your fulfillment" (author's paraphrase). Footwashing, though often neglected, is still celebrated in the worship life of many Christians. On the Thursday evening before Easter, Christians around the world take a basin of water, kneel, and wash the feet of one another.

As we seek to adopt the habit of serving, not just as a worship act but as a model of life, a new context is provided for everything we do. Our work, our home, and any other place we have influence are now seen as opportunities to offer ourselves for the benefit of our neighbors. We discover that the way to thrive is to help the person in need to thrive; the way for us to flourish is to assist other people in flourishing; the way to a full life is by emptying ourselves. Our goal is no longer to expand ourselves through power, prestige, and possessions but to pour out all these things as did the Samaritan beside the road. We empty ourselves following Christ, who emptied himself for us. This style of life makes concrete the second part of Jesus' Great Commandment, "Love your neighbor as yourself" (Luke 10:27).

WHY SERVE?

"I believe . . . that every human mind feels pleasure in doing good to another."   Thomas Jefferson

Are there advantages in serving? Is there any reward? Christians believe that people who serve are much happier than people who concentrate on getting ahead. We do lose some things by viewing ourselves as servants; being a servant rarely comes without sacrifice. Yet, in the end, those who serve generally do not wind up feeling empty. Instead, they are filled with spiritual joy. By serving other people, we end up being served by God at a far deeper level. How is that possible? The answer: A servant-attitude fulfills two fundamental human longings—to connect and to contribute.

THE NEED TO CONNECT

A fundamental human longing is the need to be part of something larger than ourselves. Christians view life in terms of the essential interdependence of human beings. God created us for communion and for fellowship within ourselves, with the people around us, and ultimately with God who created us. Conversely, a person who tries to be completely independent and self-sufficient is somehow less than whole.

At the close of Anne Tyler's novel, *The Amateur Marriage*, Michael Anton was an eighty-year old man. As Michael looked back on his life with regret, he found himself to be disconnected from the persons he loved most. Michael used to blame his ex-wife for making him feel this way. "Now he thought, it had been his own basic nature that was to blame. He was the kind who stood aloof while others waded in.... He wished he had inhabited more of his life, used it better, filled it fuller."[3]

> *"With all things and in all things we are relatives."*
> *Sioux Proverb*

When we empty ourselves for others, we establish bonds. Service breaks down the normal barriers that separate us from other people and from God. Over time, we begin to feel different—more satisfied—with our lives. We get the sense that we are really inhabiting our days to the fullest. To serve a meal in a homeless kitchen or visit someone in the hospital gets us down beneath pretenses and defenses to our spiritual heart. We experience not so much our prized separateness and self-sufficiency but our connection with other people. And in the midst of drawing closer to one another, we draw closer to the heart of the One who created us. Our service, however small it may seem, can liberate our spirit.

> *"Christ has no body now on earth but yours; no hands but yours; no feet but yours;... Yours are the feet with which he is to go about doing good; yours are the hands with which he is to bless now."*
> *Saint Teresa of Avila*

One day Mark was visiting a young wife and mother. Her husband had been killed in an automobile accident the day before.

> We talked together on the sofa in her living room, and she wondered how on earth she would manage, raising a two-year-old girl all by

herself. Just as she finished saying this, we were startled by the sound of a small motor. We stood up, looked out of her living-room window, and saw a friend from her Sunday school class. This good Samaritan was cutting her grass, walking up and down her lawn in regular rows. After that, this friend trimmed her shrubs. We watched him in silence, rendered speechless by his offering. Not once did he glance in our direction. When he finished, he loaded his lawnmower and his clippers into his truck and drove away. He never rang the doorbell. He never said a word, but his simple act reminded that young widow that she was not alone.

"[The New Testament Letter of] James considers it natural that a person of faith also has works. It is not a heavy moralistic Christian duty; it is the Christian possibility and life style."
Thomas Pettepiece

Serving another person fulfills our spiritual need to connect. Never again would that widow see her friend without the unspoken acknowledgement that on that one day he connected with her pain. Similarly, building a Habitat House with strangers builds friends. Serving a meal at a homeless shelter with acquaintances binds us together with each other and the people being served. Leading singing at a worship service unites individuals into one body. When we serve, we are never alone.

THE NEED TO CONTRIBUTE

A second primary longing in the spiritual quest is the need to contribute. Does your life really make a difference? Is the world better off for what you have done? We may often feel that if we really want to contribute, we have to do something completely different from what we have been doing: to turn our whole life upside down, empty our bank account, abandon our family and work, and commit ourselves to a cloistered religious community. Few people can ever make such contributions.

Yet, contributing may also be doing what we have always done in a new way. One manager sees his job as meeting the bottom line; another sees herself as mentoring young people in her company. A waiter may think of her job as just delivering a meal; another may see the job as making people feel at home. The Holy Spirit moves us further along in our spiritual journey when we begin to see in the small things of life that we have something unique to contribute.

When Mark was living in Germany, every Saturday morning he would wake up early, walk downtown, and have breakfast in Bonn's one and only McDonald's—his weekly dose of American fast food. This McDonald's was beside the train station that was "home" to many of the city's street people. One Saturday, Mark was very early. Hardly anyone was in the restaurant besides the staff. He recalls:

> As I was eating, I looked up and saw a homeless man sleeping in a corner booth. His head was resting on the table. Then I noticed the manager. He was walking briskly toward that table. I grimaced, wondering just how ugly their confrontation would be. But the manager walked right up to the table and set down an Egg McMuffin. The homeless man looked up. They smiled at each other like old friends, and the manager went back to his duties. Seeing that sandwich arrive was just a small act of compassion, but it revealed a different way of seeing the world. Later, I learned that this manager would arrive early to work every morning. And in a city where public facilities are in very short supply, the manager would unlock his store so persons who spent the night in the train station could use his restrooms and get cleaned up for the day.

"Do not forget that the value ... of life is not so much to do conspicuous things ... as to do ordinary things with the perception of their enormous value."   Pierre Teilhard de Chardin

How Do I Get Ahead?

What do you contribute? Not everyone can change the world, but simple acts can make a major difference in our connection with God and other people. When a racist joke is told, speak out for justice. When the signup sheet is passed, sign up. When an elderly neighbor's yard needs cutting, cut it. When the hat is passed, drop in a dollar. When a driver wants to enter the line of traffic, let her in. The list is endless. But each small action begins to change not only the ones we help; our actions also begin to change us.

WHAT IS THE PRIMARY BENEFIT OF SERVING?

Service fulfills basic human longings for connecting and contributing. In addition, service provides one more primary benefit: joy. One of the most joyful persons Mark ever knew was a woman named Lucille. It was not that she was boisterous—laughing and telling jokes. Her joy was expressed in a quiet, contained exuberance. Lucille's bright eyes, the glow of her face, her wry smile always reminded Mark of a child with a secret she could not quite conceal. Lucille died at the age of eighty-seven. Shortly before her death, Lucille revealed her secret.

When Lucille was seventy, she contracted cancer and almost died. Lucille said she prayed to God and asked for a little more time so she could devote herself to serving others. When she recovered, she spent the next seventeen years running all over her small town, helping anyone who needed her, volunteering at the local food bank, counseling persons struggling to get off welfare, assisting women recovering from abusive relationships, and sponsoring a whole host of food and toy drives. She also spent an hour each day praying for persons in crisis. One day, Lucille's cancer returned with a vengeance. The cancer spread so rapidly through her body that treatment was no use. When Mark visited her in the hospital, his emotions must have shown, because Lucille burst out, "Why are you so sad? I'm not sad. The last seventeen years have been a gift. I've had the time of my life! And God still has a plan for me. Maybe the plan is to get better. Maybe it's not. Either way, I'm satisfied."

"Saints are simply those men and women who realize that the only way to honor such a gift is to give it away."
William Stringfellow

AN INVITATION

Do you long for such deep contentment and joy? Lucille's life demonstrates that we will only find our spiritual selves by losing our preoccupation with ourselves. Joyfully connecting and contributing are gifts we discover as we serve. Yet, to find such comfort entails leaving behind a long-established habit of entitlement. As the Spirit enables us to practice serving others, we replace the old attitude of being served with a new attitude of humility and a spirited enthusiasm for connecting with our true selves, contributing to the needs of the world and re-establishing our rightful relationship with God.

In New York City, there is a plaque on the wall of the Institute of Physical Medicine and Rehabilitation. The saying (edited for inclusive language) was composed by an unknown Civil War soldier and summarizes what happens when we, either intentionally or unintentionally, serve:

> I asked God for strength, that I might achieve.
> I was made weak, that I might learn humbly to obey...
> I asked for health, that I might do great things.
> I was given infirmity, that I might do better things...
> I asked for riches, that I might be happy.
> I was given poverty, that I might be wise...
> I asked for power, that I might have the praise of others.
> I was given weakness, that I might feel the need of God...
> I asked for all things, that I might enjoy life.
> I was given life, that I might enjoy all things...

How Do I Get Ahead?

I got nothing I asked for—but everything I had hoped for.
Almost despite myself, my unspoken prayers were answered.
I am... most richly blessed!

May the Guide, who accompanies you along the path to spiritual wholeness, help you discover that service leads to joy.

---

1. Heard. No source.
2. From *Affluenza: The All-Consuming Epidemic,* by John de Graaf, David Wann, and Thomas H. Naylor (Berrett-Koehler Publishers, 2001); page 71.
3. From *The Amateur Marriage,* by Anne Tyler (Knopf, 2004); page 302.

Eight:
Can I Go Deeper Without Going Under?

The Spiritual Habit of Trusting

"Faith is not belief without proof, but trust without reservations."
                                           Elton Trueblood

Immediately Jesus made the disciples get into the boat and go on ahead of him to the other side [of the Sea of Galilee], while he dismissed the crowd.... When evening came, [Jesus] was there alone, but the boat was already a considerable distance from land, buffeted by the waves because the wind was against it.

Shortly before dawn Jesus went out to [the disciples], walking on the lake. When the disciples saw [Jesus] walking on the lake, they were terrified. "It's a ghost," they said, and cried out in fear.

But Jesus immediately said to them, "Take courage! It is I. Don't be afraid."

"Lord, if it's you," Peter [also known as Simon, one of the four original fishermen followers] replied, "tell me to come to you on the water."

"Come," [Jesus] said.

Then Peter got down out of the boat, walked on the water and came toward Jesus. But when he saw the wind, [Peter] was afraid and, beginning to sink, cried out, "Lord, save me!"

Immediately Jesus reached out his hand and caught [Peter]. "You of little faith," he said, "why did you doubt?"

(Matthew 14:22-31)

WHOM DO YOU TRUST?

Every day, we must choose whom to trust. Will the mechanic properly align our brakes? Will teachers adequately prepare our children? Will the pharmacist fill our prescription correctly? Will our significant other be faithful? When we are lost, will strangers provide the correct directions? Will the retirement home staff care appropriately for our parents? If we trust everyone, we will fall for every phony sales pitch that comes our way. If we trust no one, we will spend the rest of our lives hiding under the bed.

This daily dilemma is complicated by the crisis of trust in our culture. Following several highly publicized scandals, a *Time* magazine cover lamented: "So many choices, and no one to trust."[1] Greedy executives have damaged trust in corporations. Dishonest politicians have shaken trust in government at every level. Abusive clergy have wounded the church. When such reports accumulate, distrust spreads like an epidemic, infecting everyone in its path. Whom do you trust? In a culture like ours the question might be asked a different way: Can you trust anyone at all?

Christians have much to say about trust. They ask the question in an even more fundamental way. The questions of faith are: Where will you place your ultimate trust? Will you decide that the universe is an untrustworthy place, full of snares and dangers? Or will you choose to surrender to something larger than yourself, something that sustains and holds us all? The choice you make determines the direction of your life. To whom will you give your ultimate trust? This is the question of faith.

THE BRIDGE OF FAITH

> "*[Faith] is not a well-fluffed nest or a well-defended castle high on a hill. It is more like a rope bridge over a scenic gorge, sturdy but swinging back and forth, with . . . precious little to*

Can I Go Deeper Without Going Under?

hang on to except the stories you have heard... that it will bear your weight. All you have to do is believe in the bridge more than you believe in the gorge...."   Barbara Brown Taylor

Mark lives in North Carolina near Grandfather Mountain. This distinctive mountain rises over 6,000 feet in elevation. Not too far below the mountain's peak sways an attraction called the Mile High Swinging Bridge. This suspension bridge spans an eighty-foot chasm that rocks with the wind as you walk across. Mark recalls:

> I remember being on this bridge when I was eight years old. It was thrilling! I loved the whipping back and forth as I peered over at the gorge below. Recently, I went back to Grandfather Mountain with my young nephews. This time, the bridge was not as much fun. As we walked across that spindly little overpass, I could not help wondering, *Can I be sure the architect made all the right calculations? What if a bolt is missing or an unexpected gust of wind comes along?* Meanwhile Benjamin and Lucas felt like I did thirty years earlier. Every time the bridge started its famous swinging, they cheered as if we were on a carnival ride.

After a certain age, trust does not come easy. Each morning, we are greeted by disturbing headlines. We may also wrestle with more personal concerns as dreams unravel, relationships sour, and arteries harden. Such forces combine to whittle away whatever is left of our childlike assurance that "everything is going to be all right." When we live by faith, we attempt to recapture what we have lost. Faith is a decision to renew our childlike sense of trust.

Often, faith is seen as a commodity, something we either have or do not have. Perhaps, you have heard statements such as "She has a lot of faith" or "I wish I had a little more faith." Comments such as these may lead us to assume that faith is some mysterious quality, something a few fortunate people possess and other persons lack. Faith, however, is not something we have. Faith is something we do.

We perform faith when we place our trust in something or someone other than ourselves. We risk one more step across an unsteady bridge. Faith is a choice we make again and again.

"Every tomorrow has two handles. We can take hold of it with the handle of anxiety or the handle of faith."
Henry Ward Beecher

Over time, following the Guide over an uncertain future allows us to feel young in spirit once again, mesmerized not by the dangers of the gorge below but by the miracle of the bridge before us. Faith renews our childlike trust. It provides us with a second innocence—not the naïve innocence of childhood that trusts blindly but an intentional choice to see the world through the lens of a loving God. Faith is choosing to trust in the good intentions of the God who created us and sustains us in love, believing in the bridge more than the gorge.

Believing in the bridge is not a naïve assumption that you will always be protected from harm. Doctors still give bad news. Friends still disappoint. Loneliness still creeps in. Persons of faith acknowledge these painful realities, but they also recognize that everyone has a choice. You can focus your attention on the chasm beneath your feet or on what will get you across to the other side. To "have" faith is to choose the latter, intentionally and consistently.

GOING DEEPER

"Faith ... is like floating in a deep ocean.... If you struggle, if you tense up and thrash about, you will eventually sink. But if you relax and trust, you float.... Faith ... is trusting in the buoyancy of God. Faith is trusting in the sea of being in which we live and move and have our being."   Marcus Borg

The first followers were once separated from Jesus. They found themselves in a sailboat on a stormy sea in the midst of a major

Can I Go Deeper Without Going Under?

squall. Violent waves crashed over the bow, threatening to sink their little craft. Ancient people viewed the sea as an uncontrollable force, almost demonic in its power. In the sea chaos reigned—a cauldron of mysterious forces, an abode for horrible sea monsters. Those sailors were terrified!

The fear of Jesus' friends then turned into astonishment. The friends saw Jesus walking on the water! Demonstrating his power over the most chaotic force on earth, Jesus cowed the waves before him like an obedient dog. The swirling winds dissolved into a breeze. Jesus said to his wide-eyed followers, "Come join me on the waves. Place your life in my hands. You can trust me" (author's paraphrase).

Peter accepted Jesus' invitation. As in his first encounter with Jesus, Peter risked following Jesus' words. Peter eagerly swung his legs off the side of the boat and began traveling across the heaving waves as if he were walking down a city street. Looking into the face of Christ, Peter did the impossible, moving toward Jesus step by step on top on the water. Then, a sudden gust of wind broke the spell. Peter was reminded in an instant that what he was doing was impossible. Peter lost his focus, dropped his gaze from the steadying eyes of Christ, and found himself sinking beneath the waves.

Mark recalls,

> I remember seeing a young mother wading in a pool with her two-year-old son. As the mother supported her son with outstretched arms, the two glided around the pool like ballroom dancers. As long as the boy looked at his mother's smiling face, the little boy was having a wonderful time, blowing bubbles and kicking small surges of waves with his feet. Yet, as his mother slowly moved into the deep end, he became nervous—anxiously searching the dark blue water below him. "You're okay," she gently reminded him. "Just look at me. Everything is all right."

Jesus may have said similar words to encourage Peter: "Just look at me and everything will be all right." As long as Peter kept his eyes focused on the face of Jesus, he was fine. With each step, he inched closer to the waiting arms of Christ. But, when a gust of wind redirected his gaze to the waves crashing around his feet, he became helpless and afraid. With outstretched arms, Jesus rushed to steady his friend. As he placed Peter back on top of the waves, Jesus asked with genuine curiosity, "What happened to your faith?" (author's paraphrase).

On the Sea of Galilee that morning, Jesus' question reminded Peter that he had a choice. We all do. Faith is not the possession of a privileged few. Faith is simply a choice to keep the focus of our lives on Jesus Christ rather than on the threat of wind or waves. This potential lies within everyone. We can discover our own capacity for trusting God by risking three new habits in our spiritual lives. First, we practice seeing the world through the eyes of Christ. Second, we celebrate each small step toward faith. Third, we embrace the unknown not as a threat but as an opportunity to go even deeper in your relationship with God. As we observe these habits day after day, we will "have" faith. We will discover how to go deeper without going under.

SEEING WITH NEW EYES

> *"To have faith is not only to raise one's eyes to God . . . ; it is also to look at this world, but with Christ's eyes. . . . We must pray to have sufficient faith to know how to look at life."*
> *Michel Quoist*

The first habit of faith begins by seeing with new eyes, the eyes of Christ. John Calvin, a Christian leader of the sixteenth century, once compared Jesus to a pair of eyeglasses. Calvin said that Jesus helps Christians to see our God, our world, and our selves more clearly. With some practice, we begin to see our lives the way Jesus Christ would see them.

Can I Go Deeper Without Going Under?

Jesus once described persons of faith as those who have eyes to see (Mark 8:18). One of the unique things about Jesus was how he saw. Where other persons saw a disgusting leper, Jesus saw a beloved child of God (Luke 5:12-16). Where other persons saw a crook and a sinner, Jesus saw a potentially good person in need of forgiveness (Luke 19:1-10). Where others saw a scruffy, unwelcoming hilltop, Jesus saw a beautiful place to commune with God in prayer (Matthew 5:1). As the story with Peter indicates, where other people saw a chaotic, terrifying sea, Jesus saw just another opportunity to place his life in the hands of God. Everywhere Jesus looked—in other persons or in the natural world or in relationships—he saw evidence of God's presence. Jesus had "eyes to see." In the words of an old Bob Dylan song, Jesus could see "the master's hand / in every leaf that trembles and in every grain of sand."[2]

Jesus saw the circumstances of his own life from this same perspective. Shortly before his crucifixion, Jesus prayed in a public garden in Jerusalem called Gethsemane (Luke 22:39-45). Jesus knew that he would soon suffer a tortuous death on the cross. A statue in the present-day garden of Gethsemane commemorates that terrible moment in Jesus' life. The statue depicts Jesus lying flat on his stomach. He stretches his arms out in front of him and buries his face in the crook of his elbows. The statue illustrates the agony Jesus must have felt. And, yet, Jesus concluded his anguished prayers saying to God, "Not my will, but yours be done" (Luke 22:42). Jesus trusted God completely. He was convinced that even though something terrible was about to happen to him, God was still in control of the world and of his life. Jesus believed that whatever would happen, he remained in the loving hands of God.

How would your life change if you began to see in the way Jesus did? if the world became a hospitable place? if strangers were potential friends? if your life was secure in the hands of God? Through the Guide, you have the power to see through God's unique perspective.

Habits of the Heart

"Our whole business in this life is to restore health to the eyes of the heart, whereby God may be seen."   Saint Augustine

One of the most popular children's books ever written is the tale of a young magician named Harry Potter. Part of Harry's magic lay in his ability to see things that ordinary humans (called "muggles") do not. For instance, the books describe a magical pub, the Leaky Cauldron, on a busy London street corner. When Harry first arrived at the pub, he noticed that "the people hurrying by didn't glance at it. Their eyes slid from the big bookshop on one side to the record shop on the other as if they couldn't see the Leaky Cauldron at all. In fact, Harry had the most peculiar feeling that only he and Hagrid [a gentle giant] could see it."[3] Harry and Hagrid were able to see this wonderful place because they had eyes to see what others could not. Their magical sight was both a gift and an accomplishment.

Such insight is also true of faith. Mark recalls,

> I have a friend who is a horticulturalist. We both enjoy hiking, and sometimes we walk together. At first, I felt impatient when we shared a hike in the woods. I couldn't understand why George slowed our progress, bending over to inspect what seemed like every other tree and bush. Every so often, George would see some rare species. He would fall to his knees, mesmerized before it like some Buddhist monk. With nothing for me to do, I would lean against a tree and wait. I simply cannot see what he sees. To my untrained eyes, it is just another scrawny green plant. From his years of study and working with plants every day, George sees something more, sometimes something remarkable.
>
> I thought of George after visiting a seriously ill woman in my congregation. Although the doctors had been unable to find a cure for her illness, Grace had recently been released after a month-long stay in the hospital. I expected to hear about her ordeal, her disappointment in the test results, her worries for the future. Instead, she wanted to talk about the way she saw God's presence all around her. Grace detected God's hand in leading her to such a fine hospital. She saw God's compassion

in the face of a young medical resident who took the time to sit on the edge of her bed, to ask questions about her life, and to smile warmly at her. She witnessed God's encouragement in a bouquet of flowers that arrived from our choir. "I am so amazed," she said, "by the way God is all around me, by the way God takes care of me."

As I drove home, I wondered why Grace could see things that in a similar situation I feel certain I would miss. Then, I recalled George—how his passion for plants and trees literally changes what he sees in the woods. Grace too has a passion. She is passionate about her faith. She prays each day. She has practiced meditation for years. She reads her Bible and shares her praise of God each week singing in our choir. Like George, Grace has a trained set of eyes. Through her spiritual habits, for many years she has been sharpening the eyes of her heart to see God in the details of her life.

ROSE-COLORED GLASSES?

"God wishes to be seen, and wishes to be sought, and wishes to be expected, and wishes to be trusted."   Julian of Norwich

Before proceeding to the second habit of faith, we may legitimately ask a fundamental question: Are Christians just seeing the world through rose-colored glasses? Are followers of Jesus Christ naively choosing to view the world merely as they wish it to be? Christians believe that Jesus not only shows us a new way to see the world and ourselves; he also reveals a new way to see God. Jesus helps his people understand that because the Creator of the universe is trustworthy, then seeing with new eyes is not just wishful thinking but clear seeing.

Jesus shows us through the Guide that our faith in God is well founded and that God is worthy of our trust. Throughout Western history, every culture shares some version of the hero saga. Joseph Campbell and other scholars have detailed this universal story. For instance, in the animated movie *Shrek,* a shy green ogre rescues a princess from a fire-breathing dragon. This movie humorously illustrates the central plot of the hero saga. A young man longs for a beautiful princess. The princess's father, the king, sends the hero on a demanding quest in distant lands. This task may not sound like the ideal preparation for marriage, but the quest enables the king to judge whether the young hero is worthy of his daughter's love. The hero must demonstrate his commitment. If the hero persists, enduring great dangers for the sake of love, then the king and his daughter may appropriately trust the hero. The princess's marriage may be blessed because the hero has proven himself worthy of her love and her father's trust. At the center of a hero saga stands a test of trustworthiness.

Yet, in the Gospels—Matthew, Mark, Luke, and John—God reverses and turns upside down the traditional roles. In the Christian version of the hero saga, the King does not send a hero on a quest, but the King goes himself to prove his trustworthiness. Through the mystery of the Incarnation (the Word of God becoming flesh), God goes off to the far country of human life. In the biblical story, the hero Jesus Christ not only faces great danger. More significantly, the hero actually dies, ultimately giving up everything for the sake of the beloved. The Bible tells the story of God seeking to win our hearts by giving us a new heart. God promises to make a new covenant. "I will put my law within them, and I will write it on their hearts; and I will be their God, and they shall be my people" (Jeremiah 31:33).

> *"So long as we imagine that it is we who have to look for God, we must often lose heart. But it is the other way about—[God] is looking for us."*   Simon Tugwell

Christians do not see with rose-colored glasses but with something akin to laser-perfected eyes, given to us through the work and life of Jesus Christ. Our trust is built upon the trustworthiness of our God.

CELEBRATE EACH SMALL STEP

Undergirded by a trustworthy God and seeing with new eyes, we turn to the second habit on the way to faith: following the Guide one step at a time. In the movie *Indiana Jones and the Holy Grail,* the archaeologist and adventurer Indiana Jones searches for the Holy Grail, the cup Jesus used to serve wine to his followers on the night before his death. Indiana finds the cave that contains the Grail and successfully negotiates every waiting trap. At last, he sees the final chamber containing the Grail, yet one more test awaits him. The Holy Grail waits on the other side of the bottomless chasm with no bridge across. How will Indiana get across the divide? Indiana decides that this chasm is a test of his faith. He takes a deep breath, closes his eyes, and steps out into the void. His faith is rewarded! Indiana's foot finds an invisible steppingstone. With each new step, another stone materializes to meet him. Slowly gaining in trust, Indiana proceeds, step by cautious step, toward his goal. Finally he reaches the other side, closer to the object of his quest.

One of the things that make a life of faith so difficult is that much of the time we are walking in the dark. We walk in darkness because not only the far-off future but also the very next moment is always unclear. Darkness is watching our parents decline in health. Darkness is when a relationship ends or a job is terminated. We experience darkness as we work to overcome an addiction or struggle with an abusive relationship. Any time we do not know what to do or where to turn, we are walking in the dark. And, whenever darkness overwhelms, progress can be at worst nonexistent or at best very slow. When we find ourselves in darkness, celebrate that the Guide leads us forward.

Christians proceed slowly and cautiously, but as Indiana Jones always found a stone to meet his outstretched foot, so the Holy Spirit causes the path to rise up. We do not receive the ability to trust God completely all at once, but with each step we find that we are closer to our goal. The early Christian leader, Paul, describes this path. Paul writes, "Our salvation is nearer now than when we first believed. The night is nearly over; the day is almost here" (Romans 13:11-12). In other words, our life, confusing as it seems, is going somewhere. God assures us of that.

Because God went on a quest to be with us and the Holy Spirit is now with us as a Guide, we never walk alone. The Gospel of John says that was part of Christ's mission. As the "Word of God," Jesus Christ came to shine a light in the darkest parts of our lives (John 1). Jesus Christ fulfills the promise found in two Old Testament prayers of the Psalms: "Even though I walk through the darkest valley, / I fear no evil, / for you are with me; / your rod and your staff— / they comfort me" (Psalm 23:4); and "Your word is lamp to my feet / and light for my path" (Psalm 119:105). These two images suggest that even when we enter dark places in our lives, God lights a path for us. God shines enough light for us to proceed.

E. L. Doctorow once said that "writing a novel is like driving a car at night. You can only see as far as your headlights, but you can make the whole trip that way."[4] This image describes faith as well. We do not have to see our final destination, just one step in front of us. Some folks never get started following Christ because they look at someone like Mother Teresa or Billy Graham and say, "I'll never have faith like that." But, faith is not an all-or-nothing proposition. We do not have to possess the faith needed to complete our whole journey immediately. We merely need enough faith to begin. Though we may repeatedly stumble or find ourselves afraid to move forward in the dark, we have the strength to keep taking the risk, to keep moving forward in faith. We trust God to lead us where we need to go.

> *"I can't point to any one time in the last dozen years I 'got' faith. There were—and are—many moments, nudges, and jolts that incubated my faith and helped it grow."*   Kathleen Norris

EMBRACE THE UNKNOWN

Finally, after looking at the world with new eyes and having taken a small step, we are called toward a life of faith by embracing the unknown. Wrapping our arms around uncertainty may be the most difficult habit of all to develop. Something inside each person instinctively fears stepping out into the unknown. Yet, part of faith is recognizing that everything in our lives is moving onward toward something new. All of life is a transition. A baby learns to walk. A teenager goes off to college. A couple gets married. Another child is born. A new school year begins. An old job ends, and a new job begins. A worker retires. A parent dies. The circle of life continues. Part of faith recognizes that the Holy Spirit not only walks with us through life but also goes before us. God awaits us around every corner. In the midst of every unknown future is the God who created us and continues to love and care for us in all the days to come.

LEAPING INTO FAITH

When we face the unknown in both life and death, what is ultimately required of us is not just stepping out in faith but a leap into the arms of God. Out on the edge, we can only proceed by trusting God with our whole selves. The hero of the divine saga has already achieved the ultimate goal. At some point we must trust the Guide who led Jesus Christ out into the desert, throughout his life, and into a glorious resurrection.

A generation ago, a Christian missionary was sent to serve in another country. She was assigned the difficult task of translating the Bible into the local tribal language. The word that gave her the most trouble was *faith*. Every word she came up with seemed to fall short. One day as the missionary puzzled over this problem, a local man came into her home. He had been working in the fields all day. Sweaty and exhausted, the man went over to a chair in the corner of the room and just threw himself on top of it. He seemingly collapsed into the chair.

Suddenly, the missionary saw her solution. "What do you call that?" she asked excitedly. "Call what?" the man replied. "What you just did. Do you have a word in your language for throwing yourself into a chair that way?" The man told her of the word in his language that means to throw one's entire weight upon something. The missionary knew that she had finally found the word she needed. When you are scared and uncertain and facing the unknown, faith allows you to throw your whole weight upon the love and care of God. Ultimately, through faith you can learn to trust God enough to close your eyes and take a running leap into the unknown and into the outstretched arms of God.

A pastor named James Van Tholen faced the final, and for most people, the most terrifying unknown of all. When he was thirty-three years old, physicians diagnosed Van Tholen with terminal cancer. Shortly before his death, Van Tholen preached a sermon where he spoke frankly to his congregation about his fears.

> Dying, said Van Tholen, means the same friends you now enjoy will still get together a year and three years and twenty years from now and you will almost never come up in the conversation. . . . Hope doesn't lie in your legacy; it doesn't lie in your longevity...or your goodness. . . . All the stuff we think will keep us alive . . . only shows us how little we have to depend on, to stake our lives on, to put our hopes in.

Yet, at that moment when he was beset by fear of the unknown, Van Tholen proclaimed, "I remembered one of the simplest and most powerful statements in the entire Bible. . . . 'While we still were sinners Christ died for us' (Romans 5:8).

"I am dying," Van Tholen concluded. "And it's hard and I hate it and I'm frightened by it. But there is hope, an unshakable hope. . . . I hope in God . . . reaching out for an enemy, saving a sinner, dying for the weak. And that I can stake my life on. I must. And so must you."[5]

Can I Go Deeper Without Going Under?

SAYING YES

Guided by the Holy Spirit, as we begin to cultivate faith through spiritual habits—seeing with the eyes of Christ, taking each small step, and ultimately trusting God enough to leap into the unknown—we begin to clear away some of the distrust in our lives and make way for something new. As a poem by Michel Quoist suggests, fear and distrust will persist, but over time trusting God becomes a natural part of our lives of faith. Like Peter on the Sea of Galilee, we learn to lean on our Savior Jesus Christ, who is the One in whom we may place our ultimate trust.

> I am afraid of saying "Yes," Lord.
> Where will you take me?...
> I am afraid of the "yes" that entails other "yeses."
> And yet I am not at peace.
> You pursue me, Lord, you besiege me.
> I seek out the din [a flood of loud noises] for fear of hearing you,
> but in a moment of silence you slip through.
> I turn from the road, for I have caught sight of you,
> but at the end of the path you are there awaiting me.[6]

---

1. From *Time* (January 28, 2002).

2. From *And Now I See: A Theology of Transformation*, by Robert Barron (Crossroad, 1998); page 22.

3. From *Harry Potter and the Sorcerer's Stone*, by J. K. Rowling (Scholastic, 1997); page 68.

4. From *Walking in This World: The Practical Art of Creativity*, by Julia Cameron (Jeremy Tarcher/Putname, 2002); page 77.

5. From *Where All Hope Lies: Sermons for the Liturgical Year*, by James R. Van Tholen (Eerdmans, 2003); pages 282–86.

6. From *Prayers*, translated by Agnes M. Forsyth and Anne Marie de Commaille (Sheed and Ward, 1963); pages 121, 123.

Nine:
What Do I Do With My Doubts?

The Spiritual Habit of Questioning

"Faith which does not doubt is dead faith."
Miguel de Unamuno

A man [spoke to Jesus]: "Teacher, I brought you my son, who is possessed by a spirit that has robbed him of speech. Whenever [the spirit] seizes him, it throws him to the ground. He foams at the mouth, gnashes his teeth and becomes rigid. I asked your disciples to drive out the spirit, but they could not."

"You unbelieving generation," Jesus replied, "how long shall I stay with you? How long shall I put up with you? Bring the boy to me."

So they brought [the boy]. When the spirit saw Jesus, it immediately threw the boy into a convulsion. He fell to the ground and rolled around, foaming at the mouth.

Jesus asked the boy's father, "How long has he been like this?"

"From childhood," he answered. "It has often thrown him into fire or water to kill him. But if you can do anything, take pity on us and help us."

" 'If you can'?" said Jesus. "Everything is possible for one who believes."

Immediately the boy's father exclaimed, "I do believe; help me overcome my unbelief!"

(Mark 9:17-24)

Faith may be described as a narrow bridge across a deep gorge. Yet the way of the Holy Spirit may not always be well anchored. The Guide may lead us directly onto a trembling overpass that sways in the wind. We may be anxious whether the bridge of faith will hold. Questions abound. Our questions, however, do not indicate that we lack faith. The bridge of faith is also the bridge of doubt. We cannot cross one without encountering the other somewhere along the way.

WHY DOUBT?

Doubt is inevitable because faith, by definition, stretches the limits of human imagination. Consider what Christians traditionally believe about Jesus Christ. A religious teacher from an obscure village in the Middle East was the Son of God. His mother was a virgin. He performed all kinds of miracles: turning water into wine, feeding thousands of people with a few loaves of bread, walking on water, and healing the lame. His death undid the power of sin. Three days later, he rose from the dead, continuing to live forevermore.

What if you read this litany of beliefs and are not so sure? If you have doubts about a virgin birth, does that mean you cannot be a follower of Jesus? If you sometimes wonder whether God really hears your prayers, will God be less likely to respond? If you question whether the mistakes of your past are truly overwhelmed by divine love, will that make God less willing to forgive you? These concerns may keep you up at night. Belief takes practice. Part of practicing our faith is coming to terms with our doubts.

> *"Doubts are the ants in the pants of faith. They keep it awake and moving."*
>   Frederick Buechner

Most people have a friend who went off to college and started to see the world in a new way. Exposed to all kinds of beliefs, perhaps she began to question her own certainties. She learned in a lecture

What Do I Do With My Doubts?

that the Bible sometimes contradicts itself, and some of the biblical events may not be historically accurate. What happened? In some cases, this new knowledge acted like a crack in the foundation. The whole edifice of her faith began to crumble, and she worried that a person with doubts cannot be a good Christian. So, rather than feel like a hypocrite, she dropped out of a community of faith. She stayed away from worship. She stopped praying. Soon, she no longer thought of herself as a follower of Jesus Christ. Sometimes the specter of doubt scares people into giving up on a lifetime of faith.

But, such crises of faith do not have to turn out this way. Doubts are not necessarily a threat to faith. It all depends on what we do with them. Doubts can just as easily lead to honest, searching questions that open new avenues of belief. Christians believe that if they continue to take their questions to God, their relationship with God will grow deeper. Gradually, their faith begins to feel not necessarily more certain but stronger and more secure.

A WORRIED FATHER

People who doubt appear throughout the Bible. If you struggle with doubts but still long for deeper faith, you may find a kindred spirit in an unnamed man from the Gospel of Mark. The man is the worried father of a desperately ill boy. When he brings his son to Jesus, he has hope that Jesus can cure this terrible disease; he has heard about Jesus' healing power. But, doubt riddles this loving father. You can hear the hesitation in his tentative request: "If you can do anything, take pity on us." Jesus responds by playfully parroting his words: "If I can! Don't you know all things are possible for those who believe?" At that moment, this father wants nothing more than to be counted as a believer. He yearns for the certainty that all things—even the healing of his son—are possible. But, deep down, he is not so sure. So, the father utters perhaps the most honest expression of faith in Scripture: "Lord, I believe. Help my unbelief." So much searching faith—so much soul-rattling doubt—all in the same breath!

Faith and doubt are Siamese twins joined in their hearts, sharing a common journey toward a truth that is always beyond their understanding. Faith is not a fortress sequestered on a hill but a slender bridge over a wide chasm. Faith is trust, not certainty. God understands. God does not expect our faith to be rock-solid. But, if doubt is an inevitable part of faith, how should we respond to its nagging presence? What are some ways we can focus our attention not on the gorge below but upon the bridge that supports our feet?

> *"It's been my finding, and the finding of many famous doubters, that the simplest prayer reiterated in the face of silence—Stand by me or Guide me on—may slowly or suddenly pry a chink of reliable light, a half-open window, a glimpse of a maybe passable road."*   Reynolds Price

HOLD ON

As fellow believers and fellow doubters, we have three suggestions. The first suggestion is simple: Hold on. Do not worry so much about your doubts that you allow them to distract you from your relationship with God. Some people become preoccupied with overcoming their doubts. They assume they must "get past" their doubting before they can get on with following Christ.

> *"Is the Lord among us or not?"*   *(Exodus 17:7)*

When John Wesley, an eighteenth-century Christian leader, was a young man, he was plagued by doubt. He practiced all sorts of good spiritual habits, yet worried constantly that his faith was not sufficient. Wesley, on a trip across the Atlantic, watched with amazement the faith of some Moravians who did not fear the ocean's storms. As Wesley worked through his doubt, he came up with a solution: "Live

What Do I Do With My Doubts?

by faith until you have faith," said Wesley.[1] Wesley's discovery may reverse your assumptions. You may think that first you have to possess airtight belief, and only then do you attempt to live out your faith; only "true believers" should exhibit habits of the heart. Experience, however, often reverses the order: practicing your faith and pursuing spiritual habits of the heart strengthen your faith. If you live faith, sooner or later you will have faith.

To have faith is to know God, but not in the typical way we use the word *know*. Knowing God is not an intellectual achievement, the way we came to know our ABCs as children. Knowing God does not require us to memorize a set of propositions such as "God is all-powerful." The Hebrew word for *knowledge* in the Old Testament, *yada,* suggests a knowledge that occurs in relationships of deep intimacy. Biblical characters are sometimes said to "know" their husbands or wives. A wife does not just know her husband in the sense of being able to identify him out of a line-up. She knows him deeply and truly because she has shared a life with him. The wife has entered a relationship of trust with her husband that grows deeper over time.

Yet, no wife ever knows her husband completely. She discovers and rediscovers him a thousand times. Each small discovery takes her deeper into the mystery of who he is; but it is never enough for her to say with certainty, "I know all there is to know." There is always something more to be discovered, some deeper mystery she has yet to experience.

Our knowledge of God is just as intimate yet even more mysterious. God is a mystery that lies perpetually beyond human grasp. All created images are inadequate. All explanations fall short. When it comes to God, news reporter Edward R. Murrow's famous saying certainly applies: "Anyone who isn't confused doesn't really understand the situation."[2]

Yet, we can know God. We can know God in a way similar to knowing our spouse or parent or a lifelong friend. We can encounter

God again and again in a relationship of trust. As our relationship matures, we will know God more deeply. We will have a firmer grasp of who God really is. Yet, our knowledge will never be complete. We will never reach certainty. When it comes to the things of God, there is no ironclad proof or rock-hard certainty. Mystery lies at the heart of the universe and the God who made it. Faith is a commitment to risk—to take another step into the unknown, to throw ourselves into God's arms.

> *"To believe and to doubt... this is for [humans] what running is for a horse."*   Blaise Pascal

Anselm of Canterbury, a twelfth-century Christian, said that we can know God only by beginning first with faith—a relationship of trust—and then seeking to understand. "I do not seek to understand in order that I may believe," he wrote, "but I believe in order that I may understand."[3] Anselm suggested that if we trust God, we are free to ask searching questions, to struggle for provisional answers to a mystery that always lies beyond us. Doubt leads to the open-ended inquiry of an honest, searching faith. Like a boater's paddle, doubt propels us forward—deeper into the mystery of God.

> *"I used to think that you couldn't go to church until you had everything settled in your mind about belief. I had defined faith as certainty; now, faith is simply my decision to proceed in a certain direction. To try it, to give it your best shot."*
>   Doris Betts

FACE YOUR DOUBT

Second, having held on, now face your doubt. If we face our doubt head-on and admit its presence in our lives, doubt will lose its power over us. Ignoring doubts and sweeping them under the carpet will fail. Someone once said: "When you're wrestling a gorilla, you don't

What Do I Do With My Doubts?

quit when you get tired; you quit when the gorilla gets tired." This wisdom applies to doubts, too. When we quit struggling and push doubt aside, then doubt is going to come back like an angry gorilla, bigger and meaner than ever! Yet, if we bring doubt out into the open, keep asking honest searching questions, and continue to wrestle with our doubts, gradually our doubts will grow weaker and our faith will become stronger.

> *"Doubt is the Skeleton in the closet of faith, and I know of no better way to treat a skeleton than to bring it into the open and expose it for what it is: not something to hide or fear, but a hard structure on which living tissue may grow."*
>
> Philip Yancey

Get comfortable with your doubts. After all, they belong to you, and they are likely to be with you for a very long time. An English professor named Mark Collins stopped picturing doubt as a menacing enemy to be feared and started imagining doubt as just an annoying friend:

> Doubt sits next to me in the pew. He reads the bulletin during the sermon with his feet propped up on the kneeler. He picks his teeth with a torn corner of the hymnal. Sometimes he snores. But every Sunday ... I turn and shake Doubt's hand. His grip almost breaks my knuckles. I envy those who are seated far away from Doubt, but I choose to come back each week, knowing Doubt will find me wherever I sit.[4]

Mark Collins recalls his own struggle with doubt:

> A decade ago, my father and I spent part of our Christmas holidays traveling in the Holy Land. I was a seminary student and felt pretty confident in my faith. One day we visited the Church of the Nativity in Bethlehem. This sanctuary is one of the world's oldest churches, and it stands above the site that many Christians believe to be the actual location of Jesus' birth. Beneath the church is a small cave, containing what Christian tradition says is the birthplace of Jesus. In

that dark cave, my father and I joined a group of Christians from different parts of the world. We sang the Christmas carol "Silent Night" together in several different languages.

It was a beautiful moment; then out of the blue the moment felt ruined for me. I was overwhelmed by doubt. I looked at that cave, and I could feel my heart sink. I couldn't get over how fragile and insignificant Christ's birthplace looked. And then I recalled the scenes I had witnessed on the way into the church: busy, dangerous street corners, two men in a heated argument, and a taxi driver blaring his horn and cursing the stalled traffic in front of him. All of a sudden, the whole thing—the whole Christian faith—felt silly to me. How could anyone believe that a little baby born in this tiny cave could make a difference in our chaotic and violent world? Even more disturbing, how could the person who came from this ancient place really make a difference in my life today?

On the long flight home, I was depressed. I found myself praying my own version of the Father's Prayer: "Lord, I want to believe. But if I am going to keep following you—if I am going to risk giving my life to you – you are going to have to help me do it, because right now I am not sure if I believe anything at all."

I wish I could tell you that the Holy Spirit immediately answered my prayer —that by the time my plane touched down in New York, I was filled with assurance. But, that isn't the way it happened. My faith did return, but only gradually. I kept going to church even though at times I felt like a hypocrite. I continued to pray even though my words did not seem to make it past the ceiling. I shared my frustration with an older Christian friend whom I admired; I was relieved to learn that doubts sometimes bothered him too. Eventually that old gorilla of doubt grew tired and released its painful grip.

This experience was painful, but it was also a wonderful gift. Through it, I discovered a deeper faith. Oddly enough, living through six months of doubt ultimately made me much more convinced about my Christian faith and core beliefs. Wrestling with my doubt strengthened my faith.

What Do I Do With My Doubts?

"We shall not cease from exploration and the end of all our exploring will be to arrive where we started and know the place for the first time."   T. S. Eliot

Agonizing doubts may goad us into reconsidering some of our most cherished beliefs—perhaps not to discard them but to discover them anew. Growth through doubt hurts. In George Bernard Shaw's play *Major Barbara,* Undershaft says, "You have learned something. That always feels, at first, as if you had lost something."[5] Yet, the journey through doubt is worth the effort. When the Holy Spirit asks us to risk searching for a more authentic truth, we may arrive at a place we would otherwise miss.

DOUBTING THOMAS

Such growth happened in the life of one of Jesus' original friends named Thomas. History remembers him as "Doubting Thomas," but that reputation is probably not fair. When we consider the full story—how Thomas came to new faith by wrestling with his deepest questions—he could just as easily be called "Believing Thomas."

Thomas's story begins shortly after the crucifixion of Jesus. The first followers had sequestered themselves in a room, huddled together in grief, confusion, and fear. Suddenly the risen Christ appeared to the frightened group. Jesus Christ breathed upon them and said, "Peace be with you! . . . Receive the Holy Spirit" (John 20:21-22). The Guide was among them! But, Thomas was absent. When Thomas returned, the rest of the disciples were beside themselves with joy. They excitedly told Thomas what had occurred. But, Thomas was not so sure. Questioning, he told the others, "Unless I see the nail marks in his hands and put my finger where the nails were, and put my hand in his side, I will not believe" (John 20:25).

"Religion isn't yours firsthand until you doubt it right down to the ground."   Francis Sayre

Why did Thomas doubt? Not because he was stubborn or unfaithful. After all, Thomas was the follower who encouraged the other followers to risk their lives for Jesus. "Let us also go [to Jerusalem]," he had said, "that we may die with him" (John 11:16). Now things were different. Thomas had placed all his hope in his teacher and friend only to watch him die, crucified as a common criminal. Thomas longed to believe, but he could not. And so he abandoned his friends and endured seven days of doubt and seven nights of agonizing questions.

When Thomas finally returned, Jesus Christ appeared once again. This time Jesus turned to Thomas and showed him the wound in Jesus' side. Jesus Christ invited Thomas to place a finger on his nail-pierced hands. These wounds Thomas had to see for himself. Jesus bid Thomas to leave his doubts behind. This time Thomas was ready. He saw. He touched. He believed. Then, Thomas fell to his knees and confessed with conviction, "My Lord and my God!" (John 20:28).

Thomas is the patron saint of all persons who struggle with doubt and faith. He believed because through the Spirit he risked seven agonizing days and nights buried in the darkness of his own doubts. When he re-emerged, he was ready to begin again. Doubting Thomas became Believing Thomas and ended his story with a beautiful proclamation of faith.

DO NOT GO IT ALONE

Finally, having held on and faced our doubts, never go it alone. Following Jesus is a team sport: Don Quixote had Sancho Panya; Frodo had Sam; and Dorothy had the Scarecrow, Lion, and Tin Man. Along with the Holy Spirit, we need friends and traveling companions to help us along the way.

What Do I Do With My Doubts?

Mark admits that he is not the most adventuresome guy in the world. Once he and a friend got in a little over their heads and learned something about doubt and faith:

> Once when I was hiking with a friend in Switzerland, we did something adventurous and really stupid. Over pizza one night, we met a local guide who offered to train us for a week and then take us to the top of the Matterhorn. That sounded like a great idea. My friend and I figured everybody would be impressed when we got back home. We were all for it, at least until the next day. That was when we took a tour of the local cemetery in Zermatt and found it filled with tombstones commemorating those people who climbed the Matterhorn, but didn't quite make it all the way back alive. True to form, I suggested that maybe we should come up with another idea. So, we made an alternative plan; but our new plan was almost as bad.
>
> Our trail guide friend told us about a trail on the other side of the mountain where we could hike to the base of the Matterhorn's peak. My friend and I would not need a guide or have to learn anything technical about climbing. I assumed we ought to be relatively safe. The next day we set off on our kinder, gentler adventure. What we didn't take into account is that this trail put us on the shady side of the mountain. The higher we hiked, the colder it grew. Then the snow started, snowing harder than I've ever seen in my life. After a while, we could no longer see the trail. We didn't know where we were or where we were going. Eventually, my friend and I could hardly see each other. All we could do was to keep talking. Because I couldn't always see my friend, I was at times following simply the sound of my friend's voice. Just as I was starting to panic (actually I started about an hour before that), my friend got us back on the trail. Soon, the storm stopped. We finally came to a spot that the guide had told us about and clouds parted. We saw the most beautiful vista I have ever seen.

In our spiritual lives sometimes we will find ourselves on the shady side of the mountain. But when that happens, we should not despair. We should stick together with our companions along the way. Follow the voices of our friends. Let them take up the mantle of belief until our faith returns. Eventually our companions will lead us to the sunny side of the mountain.

Celtic spirituality, a unique kind of Christianity from the British Isles (and especially Ireland), possesses the notion of "thin places" in the universe. At these thin places, the visible and the invisible world come into their closest proximity, places where the eternal world of God rubs against our world. The Celtic Christians believed that this intersection of the holy and profane is most likely to happen in extraordinary experiences of life—times of great joy, and also times of great suffering and despair—and especially in the company of other people. These Christians believe that at such frontiers God and human beings are most intimately present to each other. Times of great doubt can also be thin places. Even though God seems far off at that moment of doubt, God is actually most present, working within us to establish a deeper faith and a more committed relationship.

> *"Deep peace of the running water to you,*
> *deep peace of the flowing air to you,*
> *deep peace of the shining stars to you,*
> *deep peace of the Son of Peace to you."*
>
> Celtic Blessing

THIS WE BELIEVE: CREEDS

In many congregations, services of worship include a creed or statement of belief that everyone says together. The Apostles' Creed is one of the most famous witnesses of faith. The plural possessive in the word *Apostles'* indicates that this is not a statement by one apostle (one follower of Jesus) but a collective understanding by a

What Do I Do With My Doubts?

whole host of followers developed over centuries of refinement. This statement of faith comes from the beginning of the third century and, today, is proclaimed by Christians of every major denomination on every continent:

> I believe in God, the Father Almighty,
> > creator of heaven and earth.
>
> I believe in Jesus Christ, his only Son, our Lord,
> > who was conceived by the Holy Spirit,
> > born of the Virgin Mary,
> > suffered under Pontius Pilate,
> > was crucified, died, and was buried;
> > he descended to the dead.
> > On the third day he rose again;
> > he ascended into heaven,
> > and is seated at the right hand of the Father,
> > and will come again to judge the living and the dead.
>
> I believe in the Holy Spirit,
> > the holy catholic [which means "universal"] church,
> > he communion of saints,
> > the forgiveness of sins,
> > the resurrection of the body,
> > and the life everlasting. Amen.[6]

When we affirm our faith by saying such a creed with other Christians, we are not merely subscribing to a catalog of beliefs. We are making a promise. The word *believe* comes from the Old English *belove*, making clear that this creed is heart language of a whole body of believers. This affirmation is a form of commitment or a vow. As a young Christian author named Lauren Winner puts it, "Saying the Creed is like vowing to love your bride forever and ever. That vow is not a promise to feel goopy and smitten every morning for the rest of your life. It is a promise to live love, even especially when you don't feel anything other than annoyance and disdain."[7]

When Christians say a creed together, we are promising to continue loving and trusting God even though we have persistent doubts, even though we may not feel a sense of certainty in our hearts.

> *" 'I believe in God' does not state an opinion or express an attitude; it makes a promise."*   Nicholas Lash

FROM CERTAINTY TO QUESTIONING

Doubt need not be seen as the spiritual equivalent of a terminal disease. The Holy Spirit leads us both to desert places and times of celebration, as we journey alone and with other people. Questioning is simply part of the journey. We can hold on to the faith we already possess, refusing to give up when doubts inevitably come. We can face our doubts, honestly and openly. Finally, we can reject the impulse to muddle through an intense period of doubting on our own and hold the hand of another. If we do these three things, the Guide will allow us to let go of our anxious need for certainty. Because God is a mystery beyond human comprehension, complete and lasting certainty about God is an illusion. We need not be intimidated by the apparent certainty of others. Those persons who try to project an air of spiritual sureness and demand it from others probably feel more than a little anxious themselves. Overly confident Christians may be overcompensating out of fear that if doubt ever creeps into their hearts, their whole faith will begin to crumble.

Instead, questions of faith, even when they lead us to struggle with doubt, are a blessing. They come from a place deep inside of us. When we risk sharing this deep part of who we are with God, our relationship with God grows stronger. The Guide leads us to become more honest with God. Questioning our faith is a vital part of an authentic spirituality—a worthy path in our quest. Faith is not the absence of doubt; it is having the courage to risk one more step into the unknown. Questioning is an act of faith—an honest expression of our longing to know the truth.

What Do I Do With My Doubts?

The German mystic and poet, Rainer Maria Rilke, once offered this advice:

> Have patience with everything unresolved in your heart and try to love the questions themselves.... Don't search for answers... because you would not be able to live them. Live the questions now. Perhaps then, someday far in the future you will gradually, without even noticing it, live your way into the answer."[8]

Live your questions. Follow the example of the unnamed father. That father's honest doubts did not keep Jesus from healing his son. Thomas also moved from doubt to faith. His anguished questioning did not prevent Jesus from loving him, nor did it keep Thomas from ultimately affirming his faith. Each of these two followers and many, many other followers, all in their own way, gradually lived their way into an answer. And, if you keep questioning, in your own way, you will discover your own answers to your deepest questions of faith.

---

1. From *Living Faith While Holding Doubts*, by Martin Copenhaver (Pilgrim Press, 1989); page 43.

2. From *The Art of the Moment: Simple Ways to Get the Most from Life*, by Veronique Vienne (Clarkson Potter, 2002); page 75.

3. From *Proslogion* (1077), by Saint Anselm, in *In a Dark Wood: Journeys of Faith and Doubt*, edited by Linda Jones and Sophie Stanes (Fortress Press, 2004); page 153.

4. From *On the Road to Emmaus: Stories of Faith, Doubt, and Change*, by Mark Collins (Liguori Press, 1994); page 79.

5. From *Living Faith While Holding Doubts*, by Martin Copenhaer; page 31.

6. From *English Language Liturgical Consultation*, 1275 "K" Street, NW, #1202, Washington, D.C. 2005-4097, revision of ICET translation. This is the translation now found in almost every official liturgical book and used in many English-speaking congregations around the world.

7. From *Girl Meets God: On the Path to a Spiritual Life*, by Lauren F. Winner (Algonquin Books, 2002); page 269.

8. From *Letters to a Young Poet,* translated by Stephen Mitchell (Modern Library, 2001); pages 34–35.

Ten: Can a Change in Me Change the World?

The Spiritual Habit of Engaging

"Be the change you want to see in the world."
Mahatma Gandhi

A few days later, when Jesus again entered Capernaum [a small fishing village on the northern shore of the Sea of Galilee], the people heard that [Jesus] had come home. They gathered in such large numbers that there was no room left, not even outside the door, and [Jesus] preached the word to them. Some men came, bringing to [Jesus] a paralyzed man, carried by four of them. Since they could not get him to Jesus because of the crowd, they made an opening in the roof above Jesus by digging through it and then lowered the mat the man was lying on. When Jesus saw their faith, he said to the paralyzed man, "Son, your sins are forgiven." . . .

[Jesus] said to the man, "I tell you, get up, take your mat and go home." [The paralyzed man] got up, took his mat and walked out in full view of them all. This amazed everyone and they praised God, saying, "We have never seen anything like this!"
(Mark 2:1-12, excerpts)

THE BUTTERFLY EFFECT

Intricate webs of relationship link all of life together. This truth is sometimes called "the butterfly effect." This concept goes back to a famous mathematician named Lorenz Attractor. Attractor demonstrated mathematically how one seemingly insignificant action has unimagined power. Attractor's discovery lead to a seemingly odd question, "Does the flap of a butterfly's wings in Brazil set off a tornado in Texas?"[1] Can the answer be true? According to many scientists, the answer is yes. Small, random events can transform a whole host of events around the globe.

> *"Each small task of everyday life is part of the total harmony of the universe."*   Saint Theresa of Lisieux

When people are caught by the Spirit of God and begin to love, simplify, find balance, give, serve, and trust, change happens in their own spiritual lives and in wider and wider circles. As the Holy Spirit/Guide leads us to new habits of the heart, not only are we changed; God also begins to change the world through us.

Near the end of his life, an elderly Christian leader reflected on this powerful spiritual phenomenon. "When I was young," he said, "I wanted to change the world, but the world did not want to be changed. So, in discouragement, I decided to change my community; but to my disappointment, my community did not want to change. As I grew older, I decided that perhaps at least I could change my family, but alas I could not. Finally, as a last resort I decided to at least change myself. And then I realized, that had I begun by changing myself, my change might have influenced my family, my family might have influenced my community and my community might have begun to change the world."[2]

You may remember the children's rhyme:

> *Little drops of water, little grains of sand,*
> *Make the mighty ocean and the pleasant land.*
>   (Source unknown)

Can a Change in Me Change the World?

One little drop of water, then another and another eventually make a mighty body of water. One grain of sand, then another and another over time create a sandy beach. One new habit and another and another may one day transform our world. Once we see this truth, our old, habitual way of seeing the world begins to change. We no longer assume that we cannot make a difference. We see that every good act becomes an entry point into something much bigger. Each small act opens a hidden door with infinite possibilities.

A STORY OF TRANSFORMATION

As related in the story about Jesus that we just read, Jesus had just begun his ministry, and it was often characterized by miraculous healings. The Holy Spirit had empowered Jesus to exorcize unclean spirits from a man, heal a woman with a fever, drive out demons, and cure leprosy (Mark 1:21-45). Jesus was now staying in the small fishing village of Capernaum, his headquarters on the northern shore of the Sea of Galilee. Persons broken in body, mind, and spirit crowded around Jesus to feel his healing touch: parents with sick children, folk with shattered spirits, the blind, lame, and possessed, and women and men with every other form of unhealthy life. Like persons who take loved ones to exclusive clinics for exotic cures or fly across the country for the latest therapy at a teaching hospital, everyone who needed special help had arrived. To picture the scene, imagine the chaos and energy in a revival service at a local arena with a television healer.

A few people in particular had a paralyzed friend who needed Jesus' healing touch. The paralytic lay around each day, depending on other people to provide food, water, and other essentials of life. His friends wanted to change his life. These friends carried their paralyzed neighbor to the home in Capernaum where Jesus was staying. These friends risked the ridicule of other people in their community for even suggesting that Jesus could help their friend. Yet, these friends knew his pain and yearned for him to be well, and they were caught up in the Spirit of God. Love overcame their fear and doubts. Their journey by foot would have been arduous; carrying a man in a stretcher was no easy task. The roads to Capernaum were steep and rocky. The friends would have been exhausted by the time they got to the house. But when they arrived, no one would allow them through the crowd to get to Jesus. "Get out of here! We were here first! Wait your turn!"

The friends, however, were not to be denied. Houses in those days were small, two-storied, dark living spaces created of lumber, sticks, and dried mud. Animals lived in the basement, people on a second floor. Many homes had an outside flight of steps leading to a flat roof where persons could sleep outdoors in warm weather. The friends risked initiating an "extreme makeover" of the home by adding a body-sized skylight, sort of a "Trading Spaces" without permission. They borrowed some tools and rope, climbed those outside stairs to the roof of the house, and began to tear through the ceiling. Digging through tiles, clay, and sticks, they created an opening in the roof. Sunlight poured into the room below. Then the sunlight was blocked as the friends lowered the paralyzed man down to Jesus.

"Come on, Mr. Frodo. I can't carry it [the ring] for you. But I can carry you." *Samwise Gamgee*

The miracle of transformation continued. Jesus saw the faith, the persistence, the love, and the passion of the friends. Nowhere does the story tell us about the paralyzed man's faith or his actions. Instead, Jesus saw the intense and tenacious efforts of the friends. When Jesus saw the faith and love of the friends, he acted. The story concludes when Jesus spoke to the paralytic, and then the former paralytic stood up, picked up his stretcher, and walked out the door. Four friends changed the life of the paralyzed man forever. The Bible, however, never says who repaired the hole in the roof!

Can a Change in Me Change the World?

JESUS WHO CHANGED US

Christians believe that one man fundamentally changed the world: Jesus Christ. Jesus Christ's birth, teaching, actions, death, and life beyond death changed forever our own personal relationship with God, how we live in community with other people, and how we interact with all of God's creation. The world is fundamentally different today, thanks to the one man, Jesus Christ, and how he loved. As one author wrote:

> He was born in an obscure village
> The child of a peasant woman
> He grew up in another obscure village
> Until he was thirty
> He never wrote a book
> He never held an office
> He never went to college
> He never visited a big city
> He never traveled more than two hundred miles
> From the place where he was born
> He did none of the things
> Usually associated with greatness...
> And today Jesus is the central figure of the human race
> And the leader of human progress
> All the armies that have ever marched
> All the parliaments that have ever sat
> All the kings that ever reigned put together
> Have not affected the life of people on earth
> As powerfully as that one solitary life.[3]
>
> James Allan

Because of Jesus, our simple acts that imitate him initiate small changes that may transform the world. Those first fishermen followers, Simon Peter and Andrew, risked following Jesus and being caught up in the Spirit of God, and they altered the shape of human history. Despite their doubts and weaknesses, they were among the first people to see the resurrected Jesus Christ (Luke 24:36-43). Each fisherman in his own way became a leader of the early church. They left behind their families and work, risked the ridicule of their people, and then proclaimed the message of Jesus Christ both in Jerusalem and around the world. A few simple fishermen from the Sea of Galilee truly brought the world into the net of Christianity.

> *"The serene silent beauty of a holy life is the most powerful influence in the world, next to the might of the Spirit of God."*
> *Blaise Pascal*

Following the example of those first fishermen, Christians around the world have also risked loving God and their neighbors in need. In millions of small actions, one Christian after another has worked to create churches, hospitals, schools, orphanages, retreat centers, colleges, retirement homes, food kitchens, peace projects, farms, and clothing centers. Operation Christmas Child, a ministry begun by Franklin Graham, offers children the opportunity to pack a Christmas box full of gifts for an impoverished child; and one by one children touch each other's lives. And the work begun by Jesus Christ and continued by the fishermen is not yet complete.

> *"The figure of Jesus . . . is threaded through our society and folded into our imagination in such a way that it cannot be excised. He is the mysterious ingredient that laces everything we taste, the standard by which all moral actions are finally judged."*
> *Thomas Cahill*

CAN YOU CHANGE THE WORLD?

Can one of your small actions really change one person's life? Can you do anything that will make a real difference in the world?

Can a Change in Me Change the World?

Can making a minor adjustment in your own life really transform the world into what God wants creation to be? Can the Spirit really catch you up and push you to a place you could never have imagined? Can human beings really create a heaven on earth, where everyone loves God and other people and all creation perfectly?

Christians believe that ultimately God in Jesus Christ and through the Holy Spirit will create a new heaven and a new earth. The last book of the Bible, entitled The Book of the Revelation of John, details one vision of Jesus Christ's ultimate transformation of all creation into a perfect reality. This transformation will happen in God's own time and through God's own intervention.

If, therefore, God alone will change the world, why do we have to do good? What is the value of our habits of the heart? The answer: Our spiritual habits of the heart both change us and change other people. By doing good, we become more whole, and we encourage other people to be more whole. By imitating Jesus Christ, we become more like Jesus and invite other people to be more like Jesus. As Tissa Balasuriya wrote, "In this mission we meet Jesus the Christ more fully. The more deeply we are committed to the human cause and the care of nature, the more truly we are identified with Jesus the Christ, who gave his life in service to others."[4]

BEING CATALYSTS FOR CHANGE

> *"In the final analysis, faith is not a way of speaking or even of thinking; it is a way of living. Maurice Blondel said, 'If you want to know what a person really believes, don't listen to what the person says but watch what the person does.' Only the practice of faith can verify what we believe."*   Brennan Manning

Many women and men believe they truly cannot make any difference in the world. The problems appear so big and individuals seem too small. In a universe with millions of galaxies, and billions of stars, and tens of billions of planets, what can you do to make a difference? The numbers are so staggering that you may become fatalistic, even nihilistic. Doubt and fear may overwhelm.

Yet, Christians believe one person risking being caught up in the Spirit of God can change the world. From Jesus, to Simon Peter and Andrew, to James and John, to countless other faithful followers of Jesus Christ who risk themselves in a web of love, they have been caught up in the Spirit of God that created, is creating, and will continue to create a new reality.

Lucretia Mott was a tiny Quaker woman who lived in the nineteenth century. In spite of her size, Mott was tireless and fearless in her work to abolish slavery and give women the right to vote. Her home was a stop on the Underground Railway. Often Mott's words fell on deaf ears. At the end of one of her speeches, Mott said, "The Light is available yesterday, today and to eternity. What is thee doing about it?"[5] In the modern world, where people go hungry, children die of AIDS, rainforests disappear, terrorism stalks, the temperature goes up, and the number of homeless people increases, what are you doing about it?

Jesus once asked his followers a rhetorical question: "What shall I compare the kingdom of God to?" Whenever Jesus talked about the kingdom of God, he was describing how life can be if we allow God's Spirit to work within our hearts. He answered his own question, saying, "It is like yeast that a woman took and worked into about sixty pounds of flour until it worked all through the dough" (Luke 13:20-21).

Now, this domestic metaphor may not sound like much. When we hear the word yeast, we may immediately think of that nicely packaged, sanitized powder that we pick up at a local grocery store. In the ancient world, however, leaven was very different. Leaven was a powerful, potent substance; a smelly little piece of old dough added to a new batch of flour to ignite fermentation—that internal process of bubbling and fizzing by which a mysterious change takes place. Leaven had a way of penetrating flour and changing it into something new. When the people gathered around Jesus that day, therefore, and heard him say the "kingdom of God is like yeast," they understood that Jesus was talking about something small that created an unexpected, radical change. In other words, Jesus announced that the presence of God must get inside you and, through a series of internal transformations, succeed in turning you, and even the world around you, inside out.

> *"If you think you are too small to be effective, you have never been in bed with a mosquito."*   Bette Reese

Leon was a bit of leaven. Leon was a successful businessman, helping run a textile mill and then buying and selling commercial real estate. Although Leon was active in his community throughout his life, his retirement truly unleashed his potential to serve. Leon cooked meals for the homeless, built Habitat for Humanity homes, added wheelchair ramps to the homes of the elderly, and visited older members in his community who had been forgotten. When Leon was seventy-seven years old, he risked journeying to Bolivia to help build a new church facility in the Andes. For two weeks, Leon worked at 13,800 feet above sea level, digging holes through rock for the foundation of the new building. After two weeks of work, Leon and his friends had dug twelve large holes that would be used for the foundations of the projected facility. Leon will never see the finished building; the facility will take several more years to build. But Leon dug the hole for the foundation; and that foundation will one day change the lives of children, women, and men that Leon will never meet. Leon's actions prove that a change in one person can begin to change the world.[6]

CREATED TO ACT LIKE JESUS

Those friends bringing the paralytic to Jesus may be an example to you. We express love to God and other people by engaging in simple, spiritual acts that imitate Jesus Christ. Like Jesus Christ, like those friends carrying a stretcher, we can initiate small changes that make a real difference. An ancient preacher once wrote to the new Christians in the Greek town of Ephesus, "You were taught, with regard to your former way of life, to put off your old self, which is being corrupted by its deceitful desires; to be made new in the attitude of your minds; and to put on the new self, created to be like God" (Ephesians 4:22-24a). Our little loving actions, our spiritual habits of simplicity, balance, generosity, service, and trust that are attentive to God and other people, make us more like Jesus Christ.

The word *Christian* means "a follower of Jesus Christ." In other words, Christians are people who act like Jesus. Imitation is part of our spiritual nature. Within as little as forty-two minutes after birth, newborns respond to their parents and other adults by imitating their facial expressions—smiling, sticking their tongues out, and wrinkling their noses. When we see God's goodness in Jesus Christ, the Spirit inspires us; and we want to imitate Jesus in our lives. As we risk imitating Jesus, we allow the Spirit to breathe into us and make us a witness to Jesus' life and teachings.

ONE SMALL CHANGE AT A TIME

"Let me light my lamp," says the star, "and never debate if it will help us remove the darkness."

Rabindranath Tagore

In your spiritual life, a few simple actions may begin to transform you. Simply reading a verse or two of the Bible each day, offering a short prayer when you awake in the morning, uncluttering your life, arranging your weekly schedule to make time for worship, offering a gift to a congregation or charity, or inviting friends at a meal to join you in a prayer can be a small step as you follow Jesus Christ.

Can a Change in Me Change the World?

"Lasting change happens when people see for themselves that a different way of life is more fulfilling than their present one."
                                                    Eknath Easwaran

Our simple actions can have a profound effect on the lives of people around us. We all have friends who believe that they married the wrong person, or are stuck in their jobs, or whose parents pose a burden, whose children give them ulcers, whose problems seem insurmountable. Few of us alone can save a marriage, give someone a job, undo the stress of family struggles, or scale great mountains; but we can assist our friends. We can carry our friends to Jesus Christ in prayer. We can listen, give advice, provide some care, and offer relief.

Mark had a conversation with a woman in his congregation. She longed to make a difference in the lives of other people but confessed that for many years she did not know how:

> I always used to wonder what my purpose in life was. That uncertainty really bothered me. I guess I was like everybody else. I wanted something big, some really big purpose. But then after a conversation with another mother who was also going through the pain of a divorced son, I wondered: Maybe this is my purpose. Maybe it's little things like this conversation. Maybe making a difference doesn't have to be something giant. It's the little things too and how all these little pieces fit together. That's what gives purpose to my life.

*"If I can stop one heart from breaking,
I shall not live in vain."*   Emily Dickinson

What is your talent, your skill, your gift, or your potential to effect change? How are you risking love in ways that effect a change in you or in your neighbors? Where is the Spirit blowing in your life? Which of your spiritual habits of love, balance, simplicity, generosity, service, trust, and doubt can transform another person? Whether you are a teacher or an artist, a physician or a nurse, a mother or a father, a cook or politician, a scientist or IT engineer, your life affects other people.

INITIATING THE BUTTERFLY EFFECT

Wangari Maathai offered a small gesture that transformed her nation. In Kenya, Maathai planted seven trees to commemorate Earth Day in 1977. She planted the trees to highlight the world's environmental crisis, especially the destruction of her own country's forests. She decided that the simple act of planting trees would be her contribution to change. She kept planting and encouraged other young people in her country to do the same. Soon women from many villages joined her in the planting. Government foresters, seeking a solution for the devastated lands, only laughed at Maathai's efforts. No one believed that unschooled village women could make a dent in the problem merely by planting trees. But Maathai's tenacity has grown into a movement of women all over Kenya that eventually has created six thousand tree nurseries. Kenyans have planted twenty million trees. And, when Maathai was elected to the Kenyan parliament in 2003, women danced for joy in the streets of Nairobi. In 2004, she received the Nobel Peace Prize; the butterfly effect was visible for all to see.

> *"A [person] has made at least a start on discovering the meaning of human life when he plants shade trees under which he knows full well he will never sit."*   D. Elton Trueblood

The twelve-step movement—a path of twelve stages toward wholeness now followed by alcoholics, drug users, codependent persons, overeaters, and Christians around the world—was inspired by one man. Here is one description of the beginning of his ministry:

> Bill Wilson, founder of Alcoholics Anonymous, was a gifted, largely self-taught man.... He became reasonably well-to-do until the stock market crash of 1929. But alcoholism had put Wilson's life on the

Can a Change in Me Change the World?

skids long before the market crashed. Binge drinking was followed by desperate remorse and unfulfilled pledges to his wife and others that he wouldn't drink again.... When Wilson seemingly hit bottom himself, he cried out (despite his unbelief): "If there be a God, let him show himself!" After which Wilson said his room was filled with a blazing light, he was filled with ecstasy and he felt like a free person.[7]

Wilson risked challenging God, casting off into new waters, changing his own life, and sharing his experience with others. Today, twelve-step programs based on one New York alcoholic's experience have changed the lives of millions of people.

Even a child, like a small butterfly, may initiate great change. Hope Stout was a little girl who acted like leaven. She was an active member of a United Methodist congregation, who discovered the joy of serving. Hope was a twelve-year-old girl in Charlotte, North Carolina, when she was diagnosed with a rare bone cancer. The Make-a-Wish Foundation asked Hope what wish she wanted before she died. Hope replied with a question: "How many children are waiting on wishes?" Hope desired neither a trip to Disney World nor meeting a movie star but to serve other children just like her. The foundation worker replied that one hundred and fifty-five children in her area needed help. Hope then expressed her wish, "I want to help raise money to grant all their wishes." Her wish began to change the shape of her community. The foundation announced a campaign, and the community began to change. Competitive newspapers, television, and radio stations cooperated. The national press picked up Hope's story. Toddlers donated allowances. Children held a walk-a-thon. A family donated its trip to Florida. Professional football players donated equipment. Vendors sold Hope T-shirts and charms. At a "Celebration of Hope" in uptown Charlotte to raise money for her dream, 15,000 people attended. Hope died on January 4, 2004. But at her death, the community exceeded her last wish. A month after Hope's death, the foundation announced that, in her name, persons contributed over $1.5 million to assist two hundred and fifty children. A simple plea from a simple child changed the lives of many people.[8]

WHAT ABOUT YOU?

One drop of water does not make an ocean, but it is a start. One tree does not make a forest, but it is a beginning. Four friends loved a paralyzed man enough to give him a new lease on life. A few fishermen risked leaving their boats and taking up a new kind of fishing. One virtuous habit, initiated by the work of the Spirit, done in the name of Jesus, and caught by the wind of the Spirit can begin to reshape us, our community, our society, and ultimately all creation. When we become a leaven prompted by God's Spirit, transformation has begun. The saying is true: The hardest part of any journey is the first step. Yet, the truth is, we will never reach our spiritual destination without taking a first step. Are you ready to take that step? Are you ready to spread your butterfly wings?

---

1. From *www.cmp.clatech.edu/~mcc/chaos_new/Lorenz.html.*
2. From *Second Innocence: Rediscovering Joy and Wonder,* by John Izzo (Berrett-Koehler, 2004); page 166.
3. From James Allan, *www.changinglivesonline.* Edited for inclusive language.
4. From *Planetary Theology,* by Tissa Balasuriya in *The Westminster Collection of Christian Meditations,* compiled by Ward and Wild (Westminster/John Knox Press, 1998); page 357.
5. From *A Quaker Book of Wisdom,* by Robert Smith (Eagle Brook, 1998); page 119.
6. Leon Lackey, saint of Central United Methodist Church.
7. From *My Name Is Bill,* by Susan Cheever (Simon & Schuster, 2004) in *The Christian Century* (February 24, 2004); page 6.
8. From *The Charlotte Observer* (February 10, 2004); page 12A. See also *www.ncwish.org.*

Eleven:
What Next?

"The great thing in this world is not so much where we stand, as in what direction we are moving."   Oliver Wendell Holmes

Through the past ten weeks, you have joined in community with inquirers like you who have asked some basic questions about how to live a spiritual life more whole and holy. In addition, you have learned how some Christians respond to these questions with a few basic virtues that may become spiritual habits of your heart: love, balance, simplicity, generosity, service, trust, doubt, and engagement. You have risked feeling the blowing of God's Spirit, traveled in a number of different directions, and discussed your own life from a variety of perspectives. As you have discovered, there are no simple answers and many differences of opinion. At the end of the journey, it may even appear that you are simply back where you began. Yet, there are paths that each of us must follow. As the German reformer of the church, Martin Luther, once wrote:

> This life, therefore, is not godliness but the process of becoming godly, not health but getting well, not being but becoming, not rest but exercise. We are not now what we shall be, but we are on the way. The process is not yet finished, but it is actively going on. This is not the goal but it is the right road. At present, everything does not gleam and sparkle, but everything is being cleansed.[1]

Habits of the Heart

CONTINUING YOUR SPIRITUAL QUEST

Now is the time for you to consider how you will continue your spiritual quest with intentionality. How will you risk finding love, balance, simplicity, humility, generosity, service, trust, and other qualities of a Christian lifestyle in your own life? What new behaviors will you adopt? Which old attitudes will you discard? Which habits do you wish to cultivate? As Jeannette Bakke once wrote, "By participating in Christian disciplines, we live out our desire and intention to cooperate with the Holy Spirit. As we do so, we are encouraged, instructed, healed, challenged, loved, renewed, and beckoned to God and godly living."[2]

> *"Wisdom comes only when you stop looking for it and start living the life the Creator intended for you."*   Hopi Proverb

Begin by celebrating what you have already accomplished! By your participation in this study, you have already demonstrated a steadfast effort to ask serious questions of the Spirit, engage in deep dialogue, and learn from other people who are also on a journey with God. On this journey, however, be cautious; you may never arrive at a final destination. The famous preacher Billy Graham said late in his life, "I am a man who is still in process."[3] You are in process, and even more hopefully, making progress to be fully the spiritual person God created you to be.

How do you continue on your spiritual journey? Reuben Job, a bishop of The United Methodist Church, once wrote:

> Practicing a preference for God and God's will is the place to begin. That means putting God ahead of all else in our list of priorities. This is not only the way to receive direction but also the way to a joyful and faithful walk with God every day. Preference for God profoundly affects our lives. We not only receive direction but find our lives transformed as we learn to turn to God and seek to walk with God.

What Next?

. . . Begin practicing a preference for God and you will discover a growing capacity to receive and respond to God's direction of your life.[4]

We invite you to risk choosing to live a full, abundant, loving, and never-ending life with Jesus Christ. Who does not wish to have such a life? Why would we choose to live a life that diminishes us, feeds us junk food, takes us down the wrong road, or leads us in the opposite direction from where we hope to be? Yet, our society encourages us to make the wrong decision, to love ourselves first, to be out of sync, to possess more and more, to be unjustly proud of our own accomplishments, to be gluttonous of foods that do not satisfy, and the list continues. But Jesus Christ offers us a different choice: the presence of God. Each of us has a choice; now is the time for us to step out of the boat and take a risk.

"The earliest prophets and saints of this millennium have all discovered that the way of faith is not always the way of ease and comfort. Determining to follow Jesus often leads us into paths we would not choose for ourselves. To say yes to God's call requires saying no to our own voice and sometimes to the voices of persons and things we love."   *Reuben Job*

One important way to continue your growth in Jesus Christ is to remain connected with the people from your small group or class. You may have found some good, new friends and wish to continue those relationships. You may decide that your group will remain together after this study ends; and staying together is certainly possible. Some small groups continue as a weekly Bible study group or as a group that meets on Sundays in a local congregation. A week or so after your class concludes, you may wish to sponsor a reunion of your small group for a supper or lunch meeting. See who comes, and make some plans together. The goal of such a group will be to encourage one another's habits of the heart. Good small-group members often ask one another in love: "How are you experiencing risk, love, simplicity, balance, generosity, service, and trust in your life?"

"I have been to the end of the earth. I have been to the end of the waters. I have been to the end of the sky. I have been to the end of the mountains. I have found none that are not my friends."

Navajo Proverb

The Christian journey with God toward serious Christian discipleship is, of course, far bigger than this study. We believe that active participation in the life of a Christian congregation, being in community with other people seeking Christian virtue, is another sure foundation in this journey. The nurturing of your journey with Jesus will take time and care and require the ongoing Spirit of God for guidance. Remember that kissing may kindle a marriage, but cooking keeps it going. Every person, upon return from a spiritual quest, also must return to his or her own community and share what has been discovered.

In whatever way you decide to continue your journey, however, you decide to continue your quest, please do so with intentionality, knowing that Jesus Christ through the Spirit is with you on your journey toward wholeness.

FOLLOW THE ROAD

In J.R.R. Tolkien's *The Fellowship of the Ring,* the hobbit Bilbo Baggins offers this traveling song to his friends. May this same song accompany you on your spiritual journey:

The Road goes ever on and on
   Down from the door where it began.

What Next?

Now far ahead the Road has gone,
  And I must follow, if I can,
Pursuing it with weary feet,
  Until it joins some larger way,
Where many paths and errands meet.
  And whither then? I cannot say.[5]

And, as the Scottish follower of Jesus, John Hunter, once prayed:
Grant, O Lord,
  that what has been said with our lips we may believe in our hearts,
  and that what we believe in our hearts we may practice in our lives; through Jesus Christ our Lord. Amen.[6]

---

1. Quoted in *A Guide to Prayer for All God's People,* by Rueben Job and Norman Shawchuck (Upper Room Books, 1990); pages 251–52.

2. From *Holy Invitations* (Baker Books, 2000) in *A Guide to Prayer for All Who Seek God,* by Rueben Job and Norman Shawchuck (Upper Room Books, 2003); page 344.

3. From *Christian Century* (November 15, 2003); page 26.

4. From *A Guide to Prayer for All Who Seek God,* by Rueben Job and Norman Shawchuck; page 205.

5. From *The Fellowship of the Ring,* by J.R.R. Tolkien (Ballantine Books, 1973); page 58.

6. From *The United Methodist Book of Worship* (Abingdon Press, 1992); 567.

Citations

WELCOME!

Paul Gauguin, [*"D'ou venons-nous? Que sommes-nous? Oj allons-nous?"* in the original French by Paul Gauguin.]

Omaha proverb quoted in *The Soul Would Have No Rainbow If the Eyes Had No Tears,* by Guy Zona (Simon & Schuster, 1994); page 24.

Antoine de Saint-Exupery quoted in *A Turning Point: Images to Words,* by Victor Gagliardi (Gagliardi Photo Collection, 2001); page 32.

Jewish proverb quoted in *A Pace of Grace: The Virtues of a Sustainable Life,* by Linda Kavelin Popov (Plume/Penguin, 2004); page 283.

CHAPTER 1.
WHERE IS THE SPIRIT IN SPIRITUALITY?
INTRODUCTION TO THE SPIRITUAL LIFE

Hildegard of Bingen quoted in *Risking Everything: 110 Poems of Love and Revelation,* edited by Roger Housden (Harmony Books, 2003); page 15.

Lakota proverb quoted in *The Soul Would Have No Rainbow If the Eyes Had No Tears,* by Guy Zona (Simon & Schuster, 1994); page 113.

Citations

Frederick Buechner quoted in *The Christian Century* (September 11–24, 2002); pages 26–33.

From *Star Wars IV: A New Hope* as Obi-Wan Kenobi describes the Force for the first time to Luke Skywalker.

Brother Lawrence quoted in *Sunbeams: A Book of Quotations,* edited by Sy Safransky (North Atlantic Books, 1990); page 148.

G. K. Chesterton quoted in *Checklist for Life for Women: Timeless Wisdom and Foolproof Strategies for Making the Most of Life's Challenges and Opportunities* (Thomas Nelson, 2002); page 69.

Augustine quoted in *Money and the Meaning of Life,* by Jacob Needleman (Doubleday, 1994); page 168.

Pierre Teilhard de Chardin quoted in *The Death and Life of Charlie St. Cloud,* by Ben Sherwood (Bantam Books/Random House, 2004); opening page.

Ashes Transformed, by Tilda Norberg (Upper Room Books, 2003) in *A Guide to Prayer for All Who Seek God,* by Rueben Job and Norman Shawchuck (Upper Room Books, 2003); page 124.

"Who Has Seen the Wind?" by Christina Rosetti, quoted in *Blue Mountain: A Spiritual Anthology Celebrating the Earth,* edited by F. Lynne Bachleda (Menasha Ridge Press, 2000); page 37.

A Guide to Prayer for All Who Seek God, by Reuben Job and Norman Shawchuck (Upper Room Books, 2003); page 212.

CHAPTER 2. HOW MUCH AM I WILLING TO RISK? THE SPIRITUAL HABIT OF COURAGE

John A. Shedd quoted in "Sunbeams" in *The Sun* (January 2004, Issue 337); page 48.

Life Wide Open: Unleashing the Power of a Passionate Life, by David Jeremiah (Integrity, 2003); pages 121–22.

James Baldwin quoted in *In a Dark Wood: Journeys of Faith and Doubt,* edited by Linda Jones and Sophie Stanes (Fortress Press, 2004); page 17.

Citations

Audre Lorde quoted in "Sunbeams" in *The Sun* (October 2003, Issue 334); page 48.

Maya Angelou quoted from the Web site *home.att.net/~quotes exchange/mayaangelou.html*

Mary Anne Radmacher quoted in *The Sun* (January 2004, Issue 337); page 48.

Anais Nin quoted in *Walking in This World: The Practical Art of Creativity,* by Julia Cameron (Jeremy P. Tarcher/Penguin, 2003); page 51.

Saint Irenaeus quoted in *The Saints' Guide to Happiness: Everyday Wisdom from the Lives of the Saints,* by Robert Ellsberg (North Point Press, 2003); page 4.

CHAPTER 3. WHAT IS MOST IMPORTANT TO ME? THE SPIRITUAL HABIT OF LOVING

The Beatles, from the song title by John Lennon and Paul McCartney.

Margaret Atwood quoted in *Sunbeams: A Book of Quotations,* edited by Sy Safransky (North Atlantic Books, 1990); page 46.

Headmaster Dumbledore to Harry Potter, spoken to Harry when Harry was rescued from the evil wizard's magic by some unseen power, *Harry Potter and the Sorcerer's Stone*, by J. K. Rowling (Scholastic, 1998); page 299.

The Life of the Beloved, by Henri Nouwen, quoted in *Love that Works: The Art and Science of Giving*, by Bruce Brander (Templeton Foundation Press, 2004); page 124.

The Beatles, from the song title by John Lennon and Paul McCartney.

Bernard of Clairvaux quoted in *Watch and Pray: Christian Teachings on the Practice of Prayer*, edited by Lorraine Kisly (Bell Tower, 2002); page 14.

John Wesley quoted in *John and Charles Wesley* (Paulist Press, 1981) in *A Guide to Prayer for All God's People,* by Rueben Job and Norman Shawchuck (Upper Room, 1990); page 157.

Carlo Carretto quoted in *Why O Lord?* (Darton, Longman, & Todd, Ltd.) in *A Guide to Prayer for All God's People,* by Rueben Job and Norman Shawchuck (Upper Room Books, 1990); page 117.

Saint Anselm of Canterbury quoted in *The Prayers and Meditations of St. Anselm,* translated by Benedicta Ward (Penguin, 1973); page 236.

Saul Bellow quoted in *The Harper Book of Quotations*, edited by R. I. Fitzhenry (HarperPerennial, 1993); page 276.

Vincent Van Gogh in the Hall of Ideas, The Church of Christian Science, Boston.

Martin Luther quoted in *Treatise on Christian Liberty,* translated by John Dillenberger in *Martin Luther: Selections from His Writings* (Doubleday, 1961); page 76.

Memories of God: Theological Reflections on a Life, by Roberta Bondi in *The Charlotte Observer* (Feb. 15, 2004); page E–1.

Ignatius of Loyola quoted in *The Secrets of Jesuit Breadmaking,* by Brother Rick Curry (HarperPerennial, 1995); page 111.

Jewish proverb in *Sunbeams: A Book of Quotations*; page 154.

CHAPTER 4. CAN I FIND BALANCE IN A WHIRLWIND WORLD? THE SPIRITUAL HABIT OF CENTERING

Living with Contradiction, by Esther de Waal (Harper & Row, 1989) quoted in *A Guide to Prayer for All God's People,* Rueben Job and Norman Shawchuck (Upper Room Books, 1990); page 316.

The Red Queen quoted in *Alice in Wonderland,* by Lewis Carroll in *The Life You've Always Wanted: Spiritual Disciplines for Ordinary People,* by John Ortberg (Zondervan, 1997); page 83.

Joan Ryan quoted in *Affluenza: The All-Consuming Epidemic,* by John de Graaf, David Wann, and Thomas H. Naylor (Berrett-Koehler Publishers, 2001); page 38.

Citations

Nadine Stair quoted in *A Turning Point: Images to Words,* by Victor Gagliardi (Gagliardi Photo Collection, 2001); page 17.

Wayne Muller quoted in *The Simple Living Guide: A Sourcebook for Less Stressful, More Joyful Living,* by Janet Luhrs (Broadway Books, 1997); page 91.

Letters to Marc About Jesus, by Henri Nouwen (Harper and Row, 1988); page 7.

Ellen Sue Stern quoted in *Simplicity Lessons: A 12-Step Guide to Living Simply,* by Linda Breen Pierce (Gallagher Press, 2003); page 76.

Thomas Kelly quoted in *Plain Living: A Quaker Path to Simplicity,* by Catherine Whitmire (Sorin Books, 2001); page 34.

Henry David Thoreau quoted in *The Simple Living Guide: A Sourcebook for Less Stressful, More Joyful Living*; page xiii.

Saint Teresa of Avila quoted in *Great Women of the Bible in Art and Literature,* by Dorothée Sölle (Mercer University Press, 1994); page 272.

Gerard Manly Hopkins quoted in *Engaging God's World: A Christian Vision of Faith, Learning and Living,* by Cornelius Plantinga (Eerdmans, 2002); page 38. Edited for inclusive language.

The Centering Moment, by Howard Thurman (Harper and Row, 1969); page 85.

Ralph Spaulding Cushman quoted in *Masterpieces of Religious Verse,* edited by James Dalton Morrison (Harper Brothers, 1948); page 408. Edited for inclusive language.

CHAPTER 5. WHAT DO I WANT TO BE WHEN I GROW UP? THE SPIRITUAL HABIT OF SIMPLICITY

Plato quoted in *The Simple Living Guide: A Sourcebook for Less Stressful, More Joyful Living,* by Janet Luhrs (Broadway Books, 1997); page 353.

Citations

Original Shaker Hymn, a dance hymn from 1848, possibly by the Alfred Ministry and composed during the period of the "Mother Ann's Work (Revival)."

The Grinch quoted in *How the Grinch Stole Christmas,* by Dr. Seuss (Random House Children's Books, 1957).

Richard Bower quoted in *Simpler Living, Compassionate Living,* by Michael Schut (Morehouse Group, 1999); page 18.

Richard Foster quoted in *Celebrating the Disciplines,* by Richard Foster & Kathryn Yanni (HarperSanFranciso, 1992); page 28.

Brian Aldiss quoted in *Sunbeams: A Book of Quotations,* edited by Sy Safransky (North Atlantic Books, 1990); page 98.

David Crean and Eric and Helen Ebbeson quoted in *Living Simply* (The Seabury Press and Harper & Row, 1981) in *A Guide to Prayer for All God's People,* by Rueben Job and Norman Shawchuck (Upper Room Books, 1990); page 289.

Bengali Song quoted in *Less Is More: The Art of Voluntary Poverty,* by Goldian VanderBroeck (Harper and Row, 1978); page 222.

Henry David Thoreau quoted in *A Quaker Book of Wisdom,* by Robert Smith (Eagle Brook, 1998); page 57.

Robert Smith quoted in *A Quaker Book of Wisdom;* pages 60–61.

CHAPTER 6. HOW DO I KEEP MY POSSESSIONS FROM POSSESSING ME?
THE SPIRITUAL HABIT OF GIVING

Gordon MacDonald quoted in *A Guide to Prayer for All God's People,* by Rueben Job and Norman Shawchuck (Upper Room Books, 1990); page 248.

The Rule of Four, by Ian Caldwell and Dustin Thomason (The Dial Press, 2004); pages 199, 236.

Saint Augustine quoted in *Less Is More: The Art of Voluntary Poverty,* edited by Goldian VanderBroeck (Harper and Row, 1978); page 67.

Citations

Thomas Keating quoted in *Intimacy with God, St. Benedict's Monastery* (The Crossroad Publishing Company, 1994) in *A Guide to Prayer for All Who Seek God,* by Reuben Job and Norman Shawchuck (Upper Room Books, 2003); page 109.

Simpler Living, Compassionate Living, by Michael Schut (Morehouse Group, 1999); page 7.

Simpler Living, Compassionate Living; page 30.

The Selfish Gene, by Richard Dawkins (Oxford University Press, 1989); pages 2 ff.

Christin Hadley Snyder quoted in *Plain Living: A Quaker Path to Simplicity,* by Catherine Whitmire (Sorin Books, 2001); page 24.

Al-Ghazali quoted in *Less Is More: The Art of Voluntary Poverty;* page 244.

Mohawk proverb quoted in *The Soul Would Have No Rainbow If the Eyes Had No Tears,* by Guy Zona (Simon & Schuster, 1994); page 102.

Richard J. Foster quoted in *Money, Sex, and Power: The Challenge of the Disciplined Life* (Harper & Row, 1985) in *A Guide to Prayer for All God's People;* page 144.

Donald J. Shelby quoted in *Meeting the Messiah* (Upper Room Books, 1980) in *A Guide to Prayer for All God's People;* page 267.

Edward J. Farrell quoted in *Gathering the Fragments* (Ave Maria Press, 1987) in *A Guide to Prayer for All God's People;* page 289.

CHAPTER 7. HOW DO I GET AHEAD?
THE SPIRITUAL HABIT OF SERVING

Albert Schweitzer quoted in *Homiletics,* Vol.16, No. 3 (May-June 2004); page 15.

Choose Life, by Dag Hammarskjöld (Random House, 1968).

Butch Owen in *Beginnings 1* (Chapter 10 Video/DVD, "How Can I Make a Life and Not Just a Living?"

Citations

Albert Nolan quoted in *Servanthood: Leadership for the Third Millennium,* by Bennett J. Sims (Cowley, 1997); page 15. Edited for inclusive language.

W. B. Yeats quoted in *Risking Everything: 110 Poems of Love and Revelation,* edited by Roger Housden (Harmony Books, 2003); page 23.

Thomas Jefferson quoted in *Walking in This World: The Practical Art of Creativity,* by Julia Cameron (Jeremy P. Tarcher/Penguin, 2003); page 220.

Sioux proverb quoted in *The Soul Would Have No Rainbow If the Eyes Had No Tears,* by Guy Zona (Simon & Schuster, 1994); page 13.

Saint Teresa of Avila quoted in *A Guide to Prayer for Ministers and Other Servants,* by Rueben Job and Norman Shawchuck (Upper Room Books, 1983); page 22.

Thomas Pettepiece quoted in *A Guide to Prayer for Ministers and Other Servants;* page 168.

Pierre Teilhard de Chardin quoted in *Rumors of Another World: What on Earth Are We Missing?* by Philip Yancey (Zondervan, 2003); page 71.

William Stringfellow quoted in *Simpler Living, Compassionate Living,* by Michael Schut (Morehouse Group, 1999); page 58.

CHAPTER 8. CAN I GO DEEPER WITHOUT GOING UNDER? THE SPIRITUAL HABIT OF TRUSTING

Elton Trueblood quoted in *Checklist for Life for Women: Timeless Wisdom and Foolproof Strategies for Making the Most of Life's Challenges and Opportunites* (Thomas Nelson, 2002); page 19.

The Preaching Life, by Barbara Brown Taylor (Cowley, 1993); page 93.

Henry Ward Beecher quoted in *The Charlotte Observer* (January 11, 2004); page D–1.

Citations

The Heart of Christianity: Rediscovering a Life of Faith, by Marcus Borg (HarperSanFrancisco, 2003); page 35.

Michel Quoist quoted in *In a Dark Wood: Journeys of Faith and Doubt,* edited by Linda Jones and Sophie Stanes (Fortress Press, 2004); page 81.

Saint Augustine quoted in *The Saints' Guide to Happiness,* by Robert Ellsberg (North Point Press, 2003); page 171.

Julian of Norwich quoted in *Finding Faith: A Self-Discovery Guide to Your Spiritual Quest,* by Brian McLaren (Zondervan, 1999); page 178.

Simon Tugwell quoted in *The Sacred Romance: Drawing Closer to the Heart of God,* by Brent Curtis and John Eldredge (Thomas Nelson, 1997); page 69.

Amazing Grace: A Vocabulary of Faith, by Kathleen Norris (Riverhead Books, 1998); pages 32–33.

CHAPTER 9. WHAT DO I DO WITH MY DOUBTS? THE SPIRITUAL HABIT OF QUESTIONING

Miguel de Unamuno quoted in *The Most Brilliant Thoughts of All Time,* edited by J. M. Shanahan (Cliff Street Books, 1999); page 186.

Wishful Thinking, by Frederick Buechner, quoted in *4400 Quotations for Christian Communicators,* by Carroll Simcox (Baker Book House, 1991); page 105.

Letter to a Man in the Fire: Does God Exist and Does He Care? by Reynolds Price (Scribner, 1999); pages 34–35.

Blaise Pascal quoted in *To Begin Where I Am: Selected Essays,* by Czeslaw Milosz (Straus and Giroux, 2001); page 314.

Doris Betts quoted in *The Christ-Haunted Landscape: Faith and Doubt in Southern Fiction* (University of Mississippi Press, 1984); page 256.

Reaching for the Invisible God: What Can We Expect to Find? by Philip Yancey (Zondervan, 2000); page 41.

Citations

T. S. Eliot quoted in *Sunbeams: A Book of Quotations,* edited by Sy Safransky (North Atlantic Books, 1990); page 103.

Francis Sayre quoted in *Life* (2 April 1965) in *4400 Quotations for Christian Communicators,* by Carroll Simcox (Baker Book House, 1991); page 105.

Celtic Blessing (source unknown) quoted in *2000 Years of Prayer,* by Michael Counsell (Morehouse Publishing, 1999); page 75.

Believing Three Ways in One God: A Reading of the Apostles' Creed, by Nicholas Lash (University of Notre Dame Press, 1992); page 18.

CHAPTER 10. CAN A CHANGE IN ME CHANGE THE WORLD? THE SPIRITUAL HABIT OF ENGAGING

Mahatma Gandhi quoted from *home.att.net/~quotesabout/change.html*

Saint Theresa of Lisieux quoted in *Sunbeams: A Book of Quotations,* edited by Sy Safransky (North Atlantic Books, 1990); page 16.

Samwise Gamgee quoted in *The Return of the King* "MMIII New Line Productions, Inc.; screenplay by Walsh, Boyens, Sinclair, and Jackson.

Blaise Pascal quoted in *Checklist for Life for Women: Timeless Wisdom and Foolproof Strategies for Making the Most of Life's Challenges and Opportunites* (Thomas Nelson, 2002); page 43.

Desire of the Everlasting Hills, by Thomas Cahill (Doubleday, 1999); page 319.

Brennan Manning quoted in *Reflections for Ragamuffins* (HarperCollins, 1998) in *A Guide to Prayer for All Who Seek God,* by Rueben Job and Norman Shawchuck (Upper Room Books, 2003).

Bette Reese quoted in *Sunbeams: A Book of Quotations,* edited by Sy Safransky (North Atlantic Books, 1990); page 146.

Citations

Rabindranath Tagore quoted in *A Quaker Book of Wisdom,* by Robert Smith (Eagle Brook, 1998); page 108.

Eknath Easwaran quoted in *Simpler Living, Compassionate Living,* by Michael Schut (Morehouse Group, 1999); page 9.

Emily Dickinson quoted in *The Book of Virtues,* by William Bennett (Simon & Schuster, 1993); page 147.

D. Elton Trueblood quoted in *The Charlotte Observer* (January 1, 2004); page D–1.

WHAT NEXT?

Oliver Wendell Holmes quoted in *The Harper Book of Quotations,* by R. I. Fitzhenry (HarperPerennial, 1993); page 107.

Hopi proverb quoted in *The Soul Would Have No Rainbow If the Eyes Had No Tears,* by Guy Zona (Simon & Schuster, 1994); page 75.

A Guide to Prayer for All Who Seek God, by Rueben Job and Norman Shawchuck (Upper Room Books, 2003); page 69.

Navajo proverb quoted in *The Soul Would Have No Rainbow If the Eyes Had No Tears;* page 40.

Notes

Notes

Notes

Notes

Notes

Notes

Notes